Also by William H. Gass

READING RILKE

ʼREADING RILKE,

Reflections on the Problems of Translation

William H. Gass

ALFRED A. KNOPF
NEW YORK
2000

THIS IS A BORZOI BOOK
PUBLISHED BY ALFRED A. KNOPF, INC.

Copyright © 1999 by William H. Gass
All rights reserved under International and Pan-American
Copyright Conventions. Published in the United States by
Alfred A. Knopf, Inc., New York, and simultaneously in
Canada by Random House of Canada Limited, Toronto.
Distributed by Random House, Inc., New York.

www.randomhouse.com

Knopf, Borzoi Books, and the colophon are registered
trademarks of Random House, Inc.

Gass, William H., [date]
  Reading Rilke : reflections on the problems of translation / by William H. Gass.—1st ed.
      p.   cm.
  Includes bibliographical references.
  ISBN 0-375-40312-4
  1. Rilke, Rainer Maria, 1875–1926—Translating.
2. Rilke, Rainer Maria, 1875–1926. Duineser Elegien.
3. Translating and interpreting. 4. Rilke, Rainer Maria,
1875–1926. 5. Authors, German—20th century—
Biography. I. Title.
PT2635.I65Z
831'.912—dc21   98-50291
                                                         CIP

Manufactured in the United States of America
Published September 14, 1999
Reprinted Twice
Fourth Printing, May 2000

THIS BOOK IS DEDICATED TO HEIDE ZIEGLER
WITH LOVE AND GRATITUDE.

Self-Portrait from the Year 1906

The distinction of an old, long-noble race
in the heavy arches of the eyebrows.
In the blue eyes, childhood's anxious
shy look still, not a waiter's servility
yet feminine, as one who endures.
The mouth made as a mouth is, wide and straight,
not persuasive, yet not unwilling to speak out
if required. A not inferior forehead,
still most comfortable when bent, shading the self.

This, as a countenance, scarcely configured;
never, in either suffering or elation,
brought together for a real achievement;
yet as if, from far away, out of scattered things,
a serious and enduring work were being planned.

"Selbstbildnis aus dem Jahre 1906," Paris, Spring 1906

CONTENTS

Contents

POEMS TRANSLATED IN THE TEXT
OTHER THAN THE *DUINO ELEGIES*

Poems Translated in the Text

Poems Translated in the Text

ACKNOWLEDGMENTS

Heide Ziegler, to whom this book is lovingly dedicated, spent much of her valuable time and energy discussing with me the meanings of the *Duino Elegies,* giving me valuable background information, advising me on strategies, correcting many of my mistakes (impossible to catch them all), and patiently reading and rereading my revisions. This book is half hers. No doubt the better half.

I am also indebted to all those who, before me, have tried to find their way through these difficult poems, and beaten a better path . . . a path from which, so often, I fear I have strayed.

Early versions of a few of these poems were published in *The American Poetry Review, Conjunctions,* and *River Styx.* The first three *Sonnets to Orpheus,* Part 1, were published in *The Chelsea Review.* I have also cannibalized from texts published in *The Nation* and in *The Philosophy of Erotic Love,* a collection from the University of Kansas Press edited by Robert Solomon and Kathleen Higgens.

The poet himself is as close to me as any human being has ever been; not because he has allowed himself—now a shade—at last to be loved; and not because I have been able to obey the stern command from his archaic torso of Apollo to change my life, nor because his person was always so admirable it had to be imitated; but because his work has taught me what real art ought to be; how it can matter to a life through its lifetime; how commitment can course like blood through the body of your words until the writing stirs, rises, opens its eyes; and, finally, because his work allows me to measure what we call achievement: how tall his is, how small mine.

READING RILKE

LIFELEADING

Open-eyed, Rainer Maria Rilke died in the arms of his doctor on December 29, 1926. The leukemia which killed him had been almost reluctantly diagnosed, and had struck like a storm, after a period of gathering clouds. Ulcerous sores appeared in his mouth, pain troubled his stomach and intestines, he slept a lot when his body let him, his spirit was weighed down by depression, while physically he became as thin and fluttery as a leaf. Since, according to the gloom that naturally descended on him, Rilke's creative life was over, he undertook translations during his last months: of Valéry in particular—"Eupalinos," "The Cemetery by the Sea"—and composed his epitaph, too, invoking the flower he so devotedly tended.

ROSE, O PURE CONTRADICTION, DESIRE
TO BE NO ONE'S SLEEP BENEATH SO MANY LIDS.

The myth concerning the onset of his illness was, even among his myths, the most remarkable. To honor a visitor, the Egyptian beauty Nimet Eloui, Rilke gathered some roses from his garden. While doing so, he pricked his hand on a thorn. This small wound failed to heal, grew rapidly worse, soon his entire arm was swollen, and his other arm became affected as well. According to the preferred story, this was the way Rilke's disease announced itself, although Ralph Freedman, his judicious and most recent biographer, puts that melancholy event more than a year earlier.

Roses climb his life as if he were their trellis. Turn the clock back twenty-four years to 1900. Rilke is a guest at Worpswede, an artists' colony near Bremen, and it is there he has made the acquaintance of the painter Paula Becker and his future wife, Clara Westhoff. One bright Sunday morning, in a romantic mood, Rilke brings his new friends a few flowers, and writes about the gesture in his diary:

> I invented a new form of caress: placing a rose gently on a closed eye until its coolness can no longer be felt; only the gentle petal will continue to rest on the eyelid like sleep just before dawn.[1]

The poet never forgets a metaphor. Nor do his friends forget the poet's passions. Move on to 1907 now, when, in Capri, Rilke composes "The Bowl of Roses," beginning this poem with an abrupt jumble of violent images:

> You've seen their anger flare, seen two boys
> bunch themselves into a ball of animosity
> and roll across the ground
> like some dumb animal set upon by bees;
> you've seen those carny barkers, mile-high liars,
> the careening tangle of bolting horses,
> their upturned eyes and flashing teeth,
> as if the skull were peeled back from the mouth.

Bullyboys, actors, tellers of tall tales, runaway horses—fright, force, and falsification—losing composure, pretending, revealing pain and terror: these are compared to the bowl of roses. Rilke has come from Berlin, where his new publisher, Insel Verlag, has been distressed to discover that Rilke's former publisher plans to bring out *The Book of Hours* as well as a revised *Cornet*. This does not get the new alliance off to a smooth and trusting start. Moreover, Rilke is broke again. During 1906, the poet had been bankrolled by his friend Karl von der Heydt, who twice generously deposited funds in Rilke's Paris bank, but Rilke's habit of staying in deluxe hotels and eating (modestly) in expensive restaurants, his dependence upon porters and maids and trains, had left him holding nothing more than his ticket to Alice Faehndrich's Villa Discopoli on Capri. Von der Heydt sent him some supplementary funds eventually, but not before making a face. Perhaps these unpleasantries account for the poem's oddly violent and discordant opening.

> But now you know how to forget such things,
> for now before you stands the bowl of roses,
> unforgettable and wholly filled
> with unattainable being and promise,
> a gift beyond anyone's giving, a presence
> that might be ours and our perfection.

More than a bowl was set before him. Though the New Year was approaching, the island was abloom with winter roses, and Rilke's cottage, on the grounds of the villa, was covered with them.

> Living in silence, endlessly unfolding,
> using space without space being taken
> from a space even trinkets diminish;
> scarcely the hint there of outline or ground

they are so utterly in, so strangely delicate
and self-lit—to the very edge:
is it possible we know anything like this?

And then like this: that a feeling arises
because now and then the petals kiss?
And this: that one should open like an eye,
to show more lids beneath, each closed
in a sleep as deep as ten, to quench
an inner fire of visionary power.
And this above all: that through these petals
light must make its way. Out of one thousand skies
they slowly drain each drop of darkness
so that this concentrated glow
will bestir the stamens till they stand.

The rose is a distilling eye. It gathers light and filters it until the
concentration is powerful and pure, until its stamens become
erect. If the rose is not a poem, the poem is surely a rose.

And the movement in the roses, look:
gestures which make such minute vibrations
they'd remain invisible if their rays
did not resolutely ripple out into the wide world.

Look at that white one which has blissfully unfolded
to stand amidst its splay of petals
like Venus boldly balanced on her shell;
look too at the bloom that blushes, bends
toward the one with more composure,
and see how the pale one aloofly withdraws;
and how the cold one stands, closed upon itself,
among those open roses, shedding all.

And *what* they shed: how it can be light or heavy,
a cloak, a burden, a wing, a mask—it just depends—
and *how* they let it fall: as if disrobing for a lover.

E. M. Butler, whose *Rilke* of 1941 was the first biography of
the poet to appear in English, writes:

There is no doubt that roses cast a spell upon Rilke.
Monique Saint-Hélier recounts how he once sent her
some fading flowers to die with her [*sic*—Butler means "to
die in her company"], because he was going away. His
description of a vase of falling roses in *Late Poems* represents him as keeping them in his room until they were
really dead, when he embalmed their petals in books and
used them for *pot-pourri*. Rilke's roses were always explic-
itly in enclosed spaces: in death-bed chambers, in his
study at night, in rose-bowls, bringing summer into a room,
bestrewing the chimney-piece as they shed their petals.
And even in his garden at Muzot, they seemed to be clad in
pink silk boudoir-gowns and red summer dresses, like carefully tended and cherished, fragrant and fragile hothouse
blooms.[2]

The poet collects the world inside himself as the rose gathers
the light of the skies, and there he intensifies it until the phallic
element of the flower dominates the symbol. Eventually the
rose bestrews itself. Petals, like poems, leave their tree. The
beautiful unity the rose once was now becomes a fall of discol-
oring shards; yet these petals can help us see to another part of
the world as through a stained-glass window.

What can't they be? Was that yellow one,
lying there hollow and open, not the rind

of a fruit in which the very same yellow
was its more intense and darkening juice?
And was this other undone by its opening,
since, so exposed, its ineffable pink
has picked up lilac's bitter aftertaste?
And the cambric, is it not a dress
to which a chemise, light and warm as breath,
still clings, though both were abandoned
amid morning shadows near the old woodland pool?
And this of opalescent porcelain
is a shallow fragile china cup
full of tiny shining butterflies—
and there—that one's holding nothing but itself.

Later, in the August of an emptied Paris, Rilke will compose a
poem about the interior of the rose: it is first an Inside awaiting
its Outside, then a bandaged wound, at last a lake full of the
sky's reflection. When the rose is blown and the petals part,
they fill, as if fueling for the journey, with inner space, finally
overflowing into the August days, until summer becomes *ein
Zimmer in einem Traum*—a room in a dream. But it is "The
Bowl of Roses" which remains Rilke's great rose-poem.

And aren't they all that way? just self-containing,
if self-containing means: to transform the world
with its wind and rain and springtime's patience
and guilt and restlessness and obscure fate
and the darkness of evening earth and even
the changing clouds, coming and going,
even the vague intercession of distant stars,
into a handful of inner life.

It now lies free of care in these open roses.[3]

It would be tempting to organize Rilke's biography around such themes, because the themes are there: the significance of the rose, the mirror, the unicorn, the puppet, the fountain, or the pathos (as for Poe) of the death of a young woman; his increasing "belief" in animism (that all things, as well as the parts of all things, are filled with life); the notion that we grow our death inside us like a talent or a tumor; that we are here to realize the world, to raise it, like Lazarus, from its sullen numbness into consciousness; that differences are never absolute, but that everything (life and death, for instance) lies on a continuum, as colors do; that we are strangers in a world of strangers; that simple people have a deeper understanding of their existence than most, and an insight into the secret rhythms of nature. These themes are like tides that rise and fall inside him, as if he were just their bay and receptive shoreline.

Rilke's parents had lost a daughter the year before they begot René (as he was christened); hoping for another daughter to replace her, and until he was ready to enter school, his mother, Phia, got him up girlishly, combed his curls, encouraged him to call his good self Sophie, and handled him like a china doll, cooing and cuddling him until such time as he was abruptly put away in a drawer. Later, with a mournful understanding that resembled Gertrude Stein's, Rilke realized that someone else had had to die in order to provide him with a place in life.

There is a photograph of four-year-old "Sophie" standing by a table upon which, unaccountably, a black-and-white dog is crouching. Atop "her" long hair a hat in the shape we call pillbox has been rakishly placed, and her high-topped shoes rise from a strongly patterned rug as if they were part of its design. She is wearing a pleated white skirt, a white tunic with a big bow at the neck, and white socks which peek out of those shiny shoes.

His mother had aspired, when she married, to something grander than she got, though she poured cheap wine into bottles with better labels, and in other ways tried to keep up appearances. During his first year, Rilke's nurses came and went like hours of the day. His time as a toy continued. Affection, lit like a lamp, would be blown out by any sudden whim. As his parents drew away from one another like the trains his father oversaw, Rilke was more and more frequently farmed out by his mother, for whom a small boy was a social drag, to this or that relation or other carrier of concern. The child began to believe that love, like money, time, and food, was in limited supply, and that any love which went into one life would not be available to go into another.

> My mother spread her presents at the feet
> of those poor saints hewn of heartwood.
> Mute, unmoving, and amazed, they stood
> behind the pews, so straight and complete.
>
> They neglected to thank her, too,
> for her fervently offered gift.
> The little dark her candles lift
> was all of her faith they knew.
>
> Still my mother gave, in a paper roll,
> these flowers with their fragile blooms,
> which she took from a bowl in our modest rooms,
> in the sight and longing of my soul.

His mother's religiosity was always on simmer, if not on boil, but its turbulence took place, Rilke increasingly felt, in a shallow pot. "I am horrified," he wrote his lover Lou Salomé, "by her scatterbrained piety, by her pigheaded faith, by all those twisted and disfiguring things to which she has fastened herself, she who is empty as a dress, ghostlike and terrible. And that I'm her child, that I came into the world through a scarcely perceptible hole in the paper of this faded wall. . . ."

In his mother's life, Josef, Rilke's father, was the principal disappointment. He had had his hopes—to advance in the military—but even years of dedicated service proved unavailing. His upward march was slowed by frequent illnesses, so that he was eventually compelled to accept a minor bureaucratic post with a railroad, where he wore a uniform which bore no medals for valor, let alone persistence. He appeared to be surrounded by bad luck. Josef's brother Emil died of dysentery, his brother Hugo committed suicide because he had failed, at fifty-one, to advance past captain (suggesting, perhaps, to Josef what he should have done), while the eldest, Jaroslav, damned Josef with his own success, at least in Phia's envious eyes.

It was Josef who insisted that the former dollchild Sophie enter military school, where she was miserable but not nearly as miserable as Rilke would be in the myth he later made of it. It was Josef, too, who assumed that the poet the boy began to play at being was his mother's doing; yet he supported Rilke financially even after his marriage to Clara; then Josef decently died and was out of life's way, unlike Phia, the empty-garmented ghost, who remained to be encountered in foreign corners, outlasting the poet. Even at the age of forty, Rilke complains in a poem that, although he has carefully built himself up over the years, as if he were as secure as a small house of stone, his mother comes and thoroughly tears him down.

The church and the military became Rainer's north and south poles. His mother's sentimental religiosity provided him with saints and the relics of saints, while his father gave him weights to lift and lead soldiers to arrange. Both realms remained active aspects of Rilke's personality, providing his poetry with an abundant stock of malleable symbols able to enter and contribute to new contexts.

Rilke wrote harshly of his mother, but of his father's short-comings he was far more forgiving, possibly because his mother hadn't been. In "A Youthful Portrait of My Father," Rilke, as he frequently did, winds the poem around a pair of hands.

Dream-inhabited eyes. The brow as if feeling a feeling
far away. A fresh wet ring around the mouth:
smileless yet seductive.
And beneath the ropes of ornamental braid,
on the slim imperial uniform,
both hands rest calmly in the cup
which encloses the saber's hilt,
a clasp now nearly invisible, as if the distance
they were first to grasp
had dissolved them.
And all the rest so self-contained,
and teetering like a top, as if we didn't understand
that deep in its own depths it disappears.

O fast-fading photograph,
held here in my slowly fading hand.[4]

Illness became René's first profession. It brought his mother to his side, especially important to him when Josef left the household. The household . . . where hands are held and hearts are consoled. Kid, Kitchen, Kirk, Koffee in which to dip a Kookie: they add up to Komfort.

This is love, Rilke is told—and aren't we all told?—take a look: here are mother and father being nice to one another, exchanging gifts, adoring their furniture, their pets, their child; here is a faintly smiling madonna, and there a stern saint, and now a priest, to whom one is unfailingly polite, next a nurse, a friend, a dog whose tail wags; but on top of what we are told, like a cold hand, soon rests what we see and feel and finally know: the mother who picks us up and puts us down as she would a bit of knitting; the joyful union that parts, perhaps like wet paper, without a sound, in front of our fearful eyes; the cat who sings its sex in the night and runs away; those saints who swallow only candle smoke and say nothing; the dog whose devotions knock us over or dirty our pants; or the priest, with a forced warmth heating his polished face, who twists the arm of an unruly acolyte because the boy doesn't dare yelp during the service; the nurse who says "good night, sleep tight" over the closing latches of her traveling bags; and finally those friends . . . those friends who skip scornfully away to play with children who have called us dreadful names: which layer is the layer of love? is it only made of words—that kiss called "lip service," that caress called "shake hands," that welcome that feels like "good-bye"?

During childhood, contradiction paves every avenue of feeling, and we grow up in bewilderment like a bird in a ballroom, with all that space and none meant for flying, a wide shining floor and nowhere to light. So out of the lies and confusions of every day the child constructs a way to cope, part of which will comprise a general manner of being in, and making, love. Thus from the contrast between the official language of love and the unofficial facts of life is born a dream of what this pain, this passion, this obsession, this belief, this relation, ought to be.

Rilke eventually learned what he thought it was, because, when he sought a mother in his mistress instead of a mistress, leaning, as one into the wind, on Lou Salomé's spirit, she finally sent him off into the world again—out of her schoolroom, bed, and maternal hug—on account of his increasing dependency, she said, out of her need for freedom to develop, because of her similar hope on her part for Rilke and his art; and although he did not realize it all at once, he would come to understand how we constantly endeavor to match that ideology of romantic love we've been taught with the disheartening reality of its practice. Flowers fade, photographs fade, memory conspires, forgetting is a boon.

Lou Salomé was no ordinary woman. She would not be ordinary even by the standards of our time. A friend of Nietzsche's, Rilke's, Hauptmann's, Freud's, she was not, like Alma Mahler, merely a collector of geniuses (though she did collect them); she was bold, stalwart, smart, and alluring, a woman who sought her freedom as though freedom's wings would take her to the fatal flame. Gerhart Hauptmann, when they became released from whatever relation they had, said, we assume dryly, that he "was too stupid for Lou." Most were. Rilke was. Nietzsche and Freud weren't.

She was a true Muse. When she left her men they would throw themselves into the pit and subside, or into their art and succeed. She was a Muse to herself, too, producing a hundred essays and twenty books, although, as one of her biographers, H. F. Peters, remarks, as a writer, Lou "thought with her heart and felt with her head." Like a whirlpool, she drew men in, then, after a while, she flung them out again. Peters quotes one of her admirers:

One noticed at once that Lou was an extraordinary woman. She had the gift of entering completely into the mind of the man she loved. Her enormous concentration fanned, as it were, her partner's intellectual fire. I have never met anyone else in my long life who understood me so quickly, so well, and so completely, as Lou did.[5]

Rilke hated to have his mistresses go away mad; he preferred to transform ardency into friendship; but Lou Salomé was the only lover who left him before he could leave her, and this was a bitter experience which estranged them for a time. Eventually, due mainly to Lou's sagacity, she and Rilke's wife, Clara, became his closest confidants, his darlings of distance.

Lou, under the threat of Friedrich Andreas' suicide, married him (that *was* a knife he had plunged into his chest and into her horrified eyes); but she only slept with men she wasn't married to, avoiding, in her sex life, all forms of habit and routine except that one. In Lou, Rilke met his match. Meeting your match may make for a doubled flame, but it will certainly result, quite soon, in two burnt ends.

They met over tea at the Munich flat of the novelist Jakob Wassermann. At thirty-six she was ten years older than the awkward young poet who had, she told her diary, "no back to his head." In nearly everything, she was far more experienced than he—perhaps not, though, at taking tea. Or at dispatching overheated notes, which he did the following morning. *Her* father was a general; *her* family was esteemed and rich; like most well-to-do Russians *she* had a French governess, admired her father, had enjoyed her childhood. Although Lou probably never had had enough grip on a faith to say she'd lost it—since, by seventeen, when she set her cap for a popular St. Petersburg clergyman, faith was already nowhere in sight—religious matters were never far from her mind, and she made, for dogma, a natural antagonist. Pastor Gillot had a lap she sat in, and where she also fainted, offering him the opportunity to take liberties, or to demonstrate great self-control (history has drawn a curtain over which); in any case, she seduced him in short order, but only up to the point of a declaration. Caution, in an impulsive person, is always particularly significant, and caution preserved her adorer's career and earned her his help in obtaining the opportunity to study at the Polytechnical Institute in Zurich (one of the few such institutions that admitted women), where she enrolled to study that for which she had no conviction: religion and theology.

In unhealthy Rome, where Lou had gone for her health, she met the philosopher Paul Rée, and shortly his friend, the classicist become philosopher Friedrich Nietzsche. At twenty-one, Lou Salomé had the sad pleasure of rejecting both men's proposals of marriage. But she had ménage on her mind, a commune in a cottage; that way, she could keep them about, adoring and busy. She began a serious study of Nietzsche, who had just completed *The Gay Science*. Many of his ideas would later drift through Lou to land on Rilke's shore.

Nietzsche could scarcely manage one wheel, let alone function as a third, and he soon grew jealous of what he saw as Lou's imbalance of attentions. As a thinker, this fellow Rée was hardly in his class. But she didn't agree. And did he want to be merely a shareholder in a mistress? Angrily, Nietzsche drove himself away, now describing Lou, as Wolfgang Leppmann reports it in *Rilke, A Life*,[6] as "this dried-up, dirty, foul-smelling monkey with her false breasts." Lou remained with Rée for several years, during which time she turned down offers from a sociologist and a psychologist before finally accepting another Friedrich, another philologist, Friedrich Carl Andreas, whose self-infliction (which nearly killed him) did compel her to say yes.

Although Lou saw nothing wrong in going on as they had been, this triangle Paul Rée could not complete, and eventually, in despair, he left her to slide slowly out of intellectual sight. Free as ever to flirt, Lou tantalized an editor in Berlin as well as playwrights in Paris and Vienna before taking up with an exiled Russian doctor she boasted could pull nails out of walls with his teeth. Her lovers were invariably younger but not invariably of the opposite sex, and when she slipped up and became pregnant Lou disappeared from her scene for a few months to tidy

things up. Wolfgang Leppmann suggests that she probably con-
ceived a child by Rilke as well.[7]

In short, Lou Andreas-Salomé was a woman with her own
program, and a past, as Rilke began to discern it, that should
have made that program clear and their future plain. Rilke
warmly wooed this unknown woman. After he read an essay
Lou had lately published—"Jesus the Jew"—he mailed her
poems he thought congenial to her point of view. He then
arranged to meet for tea, and the morning after sent by messen-
ger a flattering line. He contrived to pop up inside her field of
view at the theater. He proposed reading a few of his recently
written "Visions of Christ," persisted to a point near impolite-
ness, then carried out his threat not once but twice. Rilke also
wrote a number of wretchedly overwrought poems in Lou's
honor, including one in which he bears a bouquet of roses
through Munich's Englischer Garten. The poem hopes she will
be motherly to the poet's flowers. Well, she would.

But Lou was not to be wooed and won by anyone, however
enamored. Nor led down another's garden path, even if rosy.
Mothering, moreover, wasn't on her agenda. Still, a little tutor-
ing, whether in bed or at the study table, could do no harm.
There'd be languages to learn, Nietzsche to ponder, cultures to
encounter, a temperament to tame and steady. If Rilke had
needed a model to guide him in his future relations with
women, he certainly would have found it in Lou Salomé, who
seduced and abandoned with migratory regularity. As Lou had,
Rilke would use marriage as a form of self-protection. And like
Lou, he would specialize in dumping.

A common problem had initiated their relation: how to give
meaning to a world that has lost its deity, and thus its purpose
and meaning. Lou would ultimately psychoanalyze the need.
Rilke would overthrow God in one set of poems and supplant
Him altogether in another.

Lou told Rilke to keep a diary, and sent him to Italy to fill it; she took him along as her lover when she and her husband traveled to Russia; she ordered him to drop René for Rainer (more manly, more German), and to change his handwriting, which, full of obedience, Rilke refashioned into the elegant calligraphy which held all his later poems.

Rilke was becoming a battered lover. He was fetched; he was sent away; more and more there was another lover present, or a husband, a critic Lou wanted to consult for an article she was writing; and there were women visitors as well whose arrival and departure he had to endure; so that he dangled when he wished to cling. They could be alone, but rarely alone together. He would sulk or (as Lou thought) grow hysterical. She endured his moods with less and less forbearance, eventually seeking the diagnosis of another lover, a physician acquainted with psychiatry, without any sense for the intolerable high handedness of her own behavior.

Rilke got his wish. Their second Russian journey would be taken without Andreas. They would at last travel to Lou's land (though she knew only St. Petersburg) and together refresh their creative spirits. Travel, however, is the severest and truest test of compatibility. After spending several weeks in Moscow and learning that Tolstoy was at his country estate, the couple set off to Yasnaya Polyana to pay the great man a visit, full of the presumption of fans who believe their adoration alone makes their idol sacred. For them, the occasion would be unique. To the great man it would be uncalled for and only too common. They arrive in late spring sunshine, a misleadingly propitious sign, and after some searching finally find a servant to carry in their cards. The count, in the middle of another prolonged quarrel with his wife, is in a surly mood. He allows Lou to enter but slams the door behind her and in front of Rilke's face—a detail Rilke omits in his own account.

The count tosses the couple into the indifferent company of his son, Sergei, who walks them about before leaving them to their own devices for much of the morning. Their devices are few in number: studying portraits, examining the spines of books. Tick . . . very slowly . . . tick. They encounter the countess, who is curt and preoccupied. After all, the Tolstoys have only recently reoccupied their summer place, and the countess is still shelving books. Finally, the great man reappears, and, instead of lunch, leads them on a walk through the garden while he speaks to Lou in a Russian too rapid and colloquial for Rilke to follow, although Rilke claims to have understood every syllable—every warm and animated word—that was not drowned out by the wind. Rilke biographer Ralph Freedman, whose revisionist version I am relying on, shrewdly sums up Lou Salomé's response: "The extent of the snub, a burden of embarrassment that seemed to have devolved from Rilke upon her, revealing him in all his inadequacy, may have hastened the end of their conjugal phase."[8]

By train, by wagon, by Volga steamer, they reached Kiev, where they stayed in a hotel which appeared to rent rooms by the hour. In Saratov, the horse pulling their cab from station to pier went wild, nearly spilling them into the street. They missed the boat. Then it was Novgorod and finally a small distant village where, in a fit of romantic overreach (which was, alas, characteristic of both), they decided to stay close to the peasants by living next to a barnyard, sleeping on—now—separate straw mattresses, suffering porridge, splinters, and large noisy flies.

Back in St. Petersburg, after only a day, Lou excused herself and went to Finland to visit her mother, leaving Rilke behind in a rooming house to howl. She stayed away a month, and then the couple—now uncoupled—came back to Berlin and regular business, which was accepting invitations. Heinrich Vogeler, whom the poet had commissioned to do the illustrations for his

Stories of God, had invited his "patron" to visit him at Worpswede, an art colony which was located in bog country not far
from Bremen—a spare flat land valued for its isolation and its
light. The trip offered Rilke much-needed relief, and he arrived,
one might say, panting. His dormer room overlooked the
kitchen courtyard. From there, like a muezzin, he called out
what the housekeeper sourly described as his prayers, and from
there he also sallied forth in his Tartar boots and Russian smock
to collect the smiles of the local peasants.

For five weeks Rilke lived quietly among creative people.
Worpswede's simplicities, its communal dedication, its serenity, enchanted him. Here he met his future wife as well as the
painter Paula Becker, whom he fancied first. Rilke kept a diary
during this time, as he had in Florence at Lou's behest. Paula
appears in it as "the blond painter." Poetic fragments and prose
sketches fill its pages. These pieces often couple roses with sex
in a commonplace way, and with death in an ominous one.
Paula's eyes are soft and warm as opening roses, he writes. Light
glistens in them as from the tips and breasts of bent petals.

Blooms, as Rilke knew, are all business; they exist for butterflies and bees, but only incidentally for us, for whom flowers are
fortuitous. Autumn's hues are even more serendipital; the function of the leaves has been fulfilled, so they are discarded, they
are finished, and their colors are the result of useless residues.
The beauty of the world happens only in our eye; even the allure
of women is as utilitarian as a wagon's wheel. The Worpswede
light, the way the countryside's colors glow even on a dim wet
evening, the festive stars and the warm windows of distant
farms, the comforting purl of a stream: those are the purest
accidents. So when one of us turns aside from living in order to
admire life; when a rose petal is allowed to cool an eyelid; when
a line of charcoal depicts the inviting length of a thigh; we are
no longer going in nature's direction but contrary to it. What

was never meant for us becomes ours entirely; what never had a use is suddenly all we need. Gradually, what Rilke's Russian adventure had appeared to teach him—how to live in harmony with nature, so appealing to the poet—would prove itself impossible for the poem.

Rilke returned to Berlin and to a Lou who had already sent him back like a bad bottle. "I wish he'd go away," she confessed to her journal. Rilke's spirit is willing: he writes to Clara every day. He plans a third trip to Russia. But his several journalistic projects, designed to bring in a few marks, are not panning out, and his accounts are empty. He meets Gerhart Hauptmann and attends a rehearsal of *Michael Kramer*, which impresses him. Rilke found distraction in the theater, as he frequently succeeded in doing during his early days, though his gifts were not suited to it. He was fascinated—in my terms—by the fake camaraderie of casts during the hubbub of rehearsals, by a play's forceful and immediate impact on its audience, the way an actor's voice could elevate the most puerile of feelings, the crude simplicities of theatrical scene setting, the art's unapologetic melodramatic formulas. Another distraction: the blond painter visits and is tantalizing, although she will soon inform the poet of her impending marriage to Otto Modersohn, while being saddened herself by his own news, some weeks later, that he intends to marry "the dark-haired sculptress." Clara? Lou Salomé is appalled. She then writes what biographers like to call her "Last Appeal." Rilke's depressions are symptoms of a sickness; his sicknesses make her sick as well; he is not to write or try to see her again; she releases him in order to release herself.

The connection between Rilke and his mother/lover was a long time breaking, but his Worpswede friendships were quick-silvery and had as many degrees as a thermometer. The rapidity with which these relations were secured can be accounted for, in part, by the cruise ship atmosphere such colonies create, but principally by the way Rilke seems simply to have thrown himself into the air and cried, "Catch!"

Clara Westhoff caught him; a cottage caught him; domesticity seemed to swaddle him, and protect him with its warmth. Love is always dreamed before it is performed, and Rilke imagined himself in soft lamplight standing before his stove preparing a simple supper for his beloved—perhaps a vegetable, he writes her, perhaps a bit of porridge. He envisions a dish of honey gleaming on the table, butter pale as ivory, a long narrow platter of Westphalian ham "larded with strips of white fat like an evening sky banded by clouds," and wheat-colored tea in glasses, too, all standing on a Russian cloth. Huge lemons, reddish tangerines, silver saucers, are invited, and then long-stemmed roses, of course, to complete this picture of quiet unanxious sensuality. We need not describe the layer of boring chores, the clutter of mismated china, sticky pots, and soiled silver, annoying habits and nervous tics, which will cloud the rich cloth when reality arrives; and the bellowing of the baby, her repeated poops, the sighs of reproach, the pure passages of self-pity which will carom from one small room to another before disappearing out the door—a poor smell seeking to improve itself by flight and dissipation.

He possesses his wife. How? By trying to make her life (as he endeavored to make his) into a sacred rite. Her friends observe it: how he has enthralled her. Whereas she first encompasses and then possesses the child. On the other hand, when the couple appears in public, the large and robust Clara seems to have her little Rilke beneath her arm (a few wrote) like a pet pooch. Routines take over. How in the world can three live as one? . . . in the same space with a pouty face, in the humorless boudoir, the barren pantry? Clara concentrates on Rilke, and her concentration compacts him. He feels himself growing hard, rind-like, remorseless.

Ich liebe dich. No sentence pronounced by a judge could be more threatening. It means that you are about to receive a gift you may not want. It means that someone is making it very easy for you to injure them—if they are not making it inevitable—and in that way controlling your behavior. It means that someone wants you as an adjunct to their life. It means that they can survive, like mistletoe or moss, only on the side where the rib was removed. It means that one way or other they intend to own you. "Let me give you a hug. I have a hundred arms." So has Siva.

Alongside the life of recurrent symbols, then—the rose and the mirror, the simple peasant and the simply plain—one might set down that of the lover and letter writer, a man drawn to women like a bee who, heavy with their honey, soon returns to his hive; or one might remark Rilke's career as a social climber, as the accomplished cultivator of those who may prove to be of some assistance to Art—occasionally artists, critics, editors, and poets, but generally people of wealth, position, and comfortable estates; or take note of the life of "the inspired one," who is attacked by the Muse from time to time the way storms lash rocky coasts—the same shores where the tides rise—with sudden stiff onslaughts of both poetry and prose. Above all, for the biographer, Rilke is the traveler who passes through places the way others pass their years.

With a romantic naiveté for which we may feel some nostalgia now, and out of a precocity for personality as well as verse, Rilke struggled his entire life to be a poet—not a pure poet, but purely a poet—because he felt, against good advice and much experience to the contrary, that poetry could only be written by one who was already a poet: and a poet was above ordinary life (Villiers de L'Isle-Adam's famous quip, "As for living, we shall have our servants do that for us," described his attitude perfectly); the true poet dwelt in a realm devoted entirely to the spirit (yes, Rilke had "realms" in which he "dwelt"); the true poet was always "on the job"; the true poet never hankered for a flagon of wine or a leg of mutton or a leg of lady either (women were "the Muse," to be courted through the post); nor did the true poet mop floors or dandle babies or masturbate or follow the horses or use the john; the true poet was an agent of transfiguration whose sole function was the almost magical movement of matter into mind.

Rilke was eventually very convincing in his chosen role. This testimony, which I take from Edmond Jaloux, could be multiplied.

> When I began talking with Rilke it seemed to me that it was the first time that I talked with a poet. I mean to say that all the other poets I have known, however great they were, were poets only in their minds; outside their work they lived in the same world as I, with the same creatures ... but when Rilke began to talk he introduced me to a world that was his own and into which I could enter only by some sort of miracle.[9]

His poetic persona may have played well even in front of the French, but Rilke was only intermittently sure of his success. Facial hair, for instance, was a problem. His father had muttonchops and a full mustache. Rilke's beard always looked young, as if it hadn't quite arrived yet, and his mustache tried to outdo itself, eventually drooping in a vaguely oriental manner. By the First World War it had lidded his mouth in the fashion of his eyes. During the years which followed, the beard disappeared, and the mustache gradually shortened itself. One could say he was wearing something conventional by the time he took up residence at Muzot, in Switzerland. But he kept the spirit well covered: long coat, hat, tie, vest, the shiny tips of his shoes showing beneath trousers bearing exclamatory creases.

The course of life was consequently marked and marred by weakness, by giving in, by disappointment, as he ate, loved, schemed for advancement, groveled for money or employment, worried about a roof over his head, while trying to keep that head in the good clouds where it belonged. There were periods for Rilke when the world seemed to want him, and he acquiesced. But friends and lovers held him, like a restive balloon, near the earth; possessions were possessive, families were like closing fists; even historic cities, sunny seaside towns, famous spas, full of charm and bent on seduction, could pull the poet into their routines, dull the eye with undesirable familiarity, and, most of all, like the whole range of ordinary things, lay claim on his time, contrive to obligate him, do him in with "duties." Money may have meant freedom, but making money was slavery. Rilke felt that everyone whose help he sought, and he had to seek help often, had been a witness to his humiliation, and so had a share in shame's hold on his sleeve—a humiliation all the more inwardly onerous if that hold had been born in nothing more than a handshake.

However, life wasn't something the poet was simply to flee from, as if it were a grave dug out of trivial routines; it was to be closely approached—approached and accepted and praised. There was, first of all, the simple life itself, the peasant's life, close to the earth, close to basic things, unspoiled by wealth and vice, unmannered and wholesome—and for Rilke the peasant's form of cleansing poverty was to be found in Russia, where he had peered in upon it. If guilt gave Tolstoy the strength to lie about "the simple life," Rilke found joyous justification in observing an existence already—by the strength of his bias— transformed for him, so that all he needed to do was describe it, since, in the peasant's fortunate union of nature and spirit, body and soul were marvelously one. Rilke liked to display his allegiance to the simple life by eating greens and taking barefoot walks.

On their two trips to Russia, Lou Salomé may have gotten something right, but Rilke was all romance, casting ahead of his every step his own dreams, into which he then strode with little satisfied cries of discovery. All of his weaknesses were awhirl: his adolescent mysticism, his wish for oneness (which evolved), his desire for a naiveté which would encompass an entire continent and keep it contained in the Middle Ages.

Poverty eventually disillusioned Rilke about poverty, but he blamed Paris for this knowledge. City poverty was horrible and crippling; country poverty remained ennobling, and its asceticism energizing. Nevertheless, Rilke preferred to stay in the best hotels and visit expensive spas. Where he'd make a meal of fruit. Solitude was the only satisfactory creative state, but communes were wonderful, standing for a common commitment: to help one another simplify life while satisfying social needs in the most acceptable way within a community of similar souls laboring for similar results. But one's fellows married (hadn't he?) and found themselves with family responsibilities (hadn't he?). They consequently turned bourgeois as certainly as souring milk; soon they only dreamt their dreams, if they entertained them at all; they became jealous, competitive, disappointed, done for, and no longer helpful to Rilke's career or a significant part of Rilke's definition of himself.

Vissi d'arte, vissi d'amore. We all feel the tug of opposing obligations, contrary desires. Rilke understood his well enough to make virtues of them. More than one poem will tell us to treat the wave of greeting as one of farewell. Rilke sent signs of his ardor safely through the post, although the passions his letters provoked were not without their hazardous consequences. Did he not tell embracing lovers to "throw the emptiness out of their arms to broaden the spaces we breathe"?—hardly an encouragement to those hungering to have him. Considering Rilke's affair with the pianist Magda von Hattingberg (whom Rilke renamed, as was his suspicious habit, "Benvenuta"), which a flurry of envelopes fanned into flames, Ralph Freedman writes: "Their life together fell into a pattern that many of Rilke's serious relationships with women would follow, beginning with sensitive caring, tender endearments, small sophisticated gifts, and an almost domestic tranquillity, before distancing set in."[10] After having convinced himself of the sincerity and depth of his feelings, the poet would overwhelm his victim with words so powerfully put together there was no resisting them. These were no longer effusions from feelings more imaginary than real, but lines linked by a thought, a music, tough as steel. *Kannst du dir den denken, dass ich Jahre so—ein Fremder unter Fremden fahre, und nun endlich nimmst Du mich nach Haus.* "Can you understand how much I've wandered, a stranger in a world of strangers, and now at last you take me home?" This is nearly irresistible. Nor does Magda manage to keep him down on the farm. Home is not where Rilke's heart is.

How I have felt it, that nameless state called parting,
and how I feel it still: a dark, sharp, heartless
Something that displays, holds out with unapparent hands,
a perfect union to us, while tearing it in two.

With what wide-open eyes I've watched whatever
was, while calling to me, loosening its hold,
remaining on the road behind as though all womankind,
yet small and white and nothing more than this:

a waving which has blown the hair beyond its brow,
a slight, continuous flutter—scarcely now
explicable: perhaps the tremor of a plum-tree
and the bough a startled cuckoo has set free."

It is the poet's purpose to put the world into words, and, in
that way, hold it steady for us. The poet can write of love, too, in
a similarly immortalizing fashion. But love alters its lovers even
as they love, so that their love is also altered and the next kiss
comes from a different mouth and is pressed to a different
breast. In this cruel yet courageous passage from "The Second
Elegy," Rilke interrogates our passions:

Lovers, satisfied by one another, I am asking you
about us. You embrace, but where's the proof?
Look, sometimes it happens that my hands grow to know
one another, or that my weary face seeks their shelter.
This yields me a slender sensation. But who dares to
      believe he exists because of that?
You, though, who, from one another's passion,
grow until, quite overcome, you plead: "No more . . ."
you, who, beneath one another's groping, swell
with juice like the grapes of a vintage year;
you, who may go like a bud into another's blossoming:
I am asking you about us. I know
you touch so blissfully because your touch survives such
      bliss,
because just below your finger's end you feel the tip of
      pure duration.
So you expect eternity to entwine itself in your embrace.
And yet, when you have dealt with your fear of that first
      look,
the longing, later, at the window, and your first turn

about the garden together: lovers, are you any longer what
   you were?
When you lift yourselves up to one another's lips—chalice
   to chalice—
and slip wine into wine like an added flavor: oh, how
   strangely
soon is each drinker's disappearance from the ceremony.

Rilke and Clara would go fifty-fifty on expenses, but the poet
had no money and small hope. His books weren't selling. By letter, he begged this acquaintance, that friend, this editor, that
institution. Little was forthcoming—a small loan, a part-time
task. He began to write reviews for a Bremen newspaper, but
few of his efforts to find such work turned into even opportunities. He was commissioned to write on Worpswede and on
Rodin—windfalls of puny fruit. And his play, *Daily Living*—
what an ironic title—had flopped as his own daily life had, at its
opening in Berlin.

Their lives passed from Clara's confinement to his . . . and
then to their union. Neither felt fulfilled, nor any longer saw the
promise of it. To Paula, Clara complained that she once could
get on her bike and simply ride away, her belongings in a back-
pack, leaving one life for another.

Rilke and his wife set one another free, then, freeing their
infant at the same time by leaving her, blanket and basket, in
the rushes of a relative. In Paris, where Rilke goes to write about
Rodin, he will learn about another kind of love—that of the
artist for his work; and about another kind of life—one in which
women are merely sources of relaxation, servants, or sometimes
models; he will learn of an existence utterly devoted to things—
things observed, things made, things preserved; but what will
strike him first is the streets and people of Paris itself, and his
profound sense of estrangement from them—of disgust, loneli-

ness, fear, despair; so that death is the topic which will pursue his pen.

Death because Paris appears to be full of hospitals, full of poor ill weak people, homeless beggars, dirt and decay. Full of city smells and city noise. The poet is no longer in the country, where there are only winds and birds. The Paris streets slowly suck him in, so that as he walks alongside them, he increasingly belongs to their flushing gutters, their screeching trams and human outcries; he leans, like others lost, against their dirty defaced walls. This is how *The Notebooks of Malte Laurids Brigge*, one of literature's great novels, begins, oozing like some wound might from the pages of his letters to Clara, who has not yet joined him. Begins with death and goes slowly on as if death will never end.

Love and death: a Germanic theme indeed. Just as going and coming are one, just as beginnings and endings overlap, so are loving and ceasing to love, living and ceasing to live, reciprocals, and as we mature our death matures, too, the way one wave rolls up the beach while another wave recedes, and each roar of the surf is succeeded by a quiet hiss.

6

O Lord, grant each of us our own ripe death,
the dying fall that goes through life—
its love, significance, and need—like breath.

7

For we are nothing but the bark and burrs.
The great death we bear within ourselves
is the fruit which every growing serves.

*

For its sake young girls grow their charms,
as if a tree-like music issued from a lyre;
for its sake small boys long to shoulder arms,
and women lean on them to listen and inspire
these not yet men to share their heart's alarms.
For its sake all that's seen is seen sustained
by change itself, as if the frozen were the fire;
and the work of every artisan maintained
this myth and made a world out of this fruit,
brought frost to it, wind, sunlight, rain.
And into it life's warmth has followed suit,
heart's heat absorbed, the fever of the brain:
Yet when the angels swoop to pick us clean,
they shall find that all our fruits are green.[12]

Rilke proclaimed the poet's saintly need to accept reality in all its aspects, meanwhile welcoming only those parts of the world for which he could compose an ennobling description. He was venomous about organized religion, yet there are more Virgin Marys, saints, and angels in his work than in many cathedrals. And he hid inside The Poet he eventually became, both secure there and scared, empty and fulfilled; the inspired author of the *Duino Elegies*, sensitive, insightful, gifted nearly beyond compare; a man with many devoted and distant friends, many extraordinary though frequently fatuous enthusiasms, but still a lonely unloving homeless boy as well, with fears words couldn't wave away, enjoying a self-pity there were rarely buckets enough to contain; yet with a persistence in the pursuit of his goals, a courage, which overcame weakness and worry and made them into poems . . . no . . . into lyrics that love, however pure or passionate or sacrificial, could never have achieved by itself . . . lines only frailty, terror, emotional duplicity even, could accomplish—the consequence of an honesty bitter about the weaknesses from which it took its strength.

> When he, whose profession was Waiting, stayed in strange
>   towns, the hotel's
> bemused and preoccupied bedroom
> morosely contained him, and in the avoided mirror
> the room presided again,
> and, later, in the tormenting bed,
> yet again—
> where this adjudicating air,
> in a manner beyond understanding,
> passed judgment upon his heart—whose beating could
>   barely be felt
> through its painful burial in his body—
> and pronounced this hardly felt heart
> to be lacking in love.[13]

Rilke's life, Rilke's poetry, Rilke's alleged ideas, have exerted an amazing attraction for many minds. It's not been just the highborn women who have sewed a skirt about him, or written him loving letters, or offered him castle space, eager ears, and ceaseless devotion; who came to him as though they were soupless and he a kitchen. Biographers have lined up to check out the contents of his life; studies have multiplied as if they had been introduced into a scholar-empty Australia; and dozens of translators have blunted their skills against his obdurate, complex, and compacted poems, poems displaying an orator's theatrical power, while remaining as suited to a chamber and its music as a harpsichord: made of plucked tough sounds, yet as rapid and light and fragile as fountain water.

Rilke was, like most men and women, many men . . . and women. How to describe this crude and jostling crowd of parvenus and office seekers without becoming fascinated or especially repelled by one or other of them, turning into a sycophant or hanging judge, as Rilke's spiritual mumbo jumbo charms, or his presumably snobby politics jars? He is passion's spokesman. He's a cold and calculating egotist, covering his selfishness with the royal robes of art. He's a poseur, a courtier, a migrant, a loner. He hates the United States for reactionary reasons: because he hates machines and commerce, and equality too. He is charming and sensitive and given to shows of concern that melt the heart. His soul is a knot of childhood resentments. He is a trifler. He is too continuously serious—he thinks of himself as a creature of myth. He has all the moth-eaten arrogance of the self-taught, and sports a learning, both quirky and full of holes, which he is as proud of as a pup just trained to paper. Put on airs? An Eskimo has not so many layers of fuss and show. A priest of the poet's art, he takes the European lyric to new levels of achievement—forming, with Valéry and Yeats perhaps, a true triune god—and creates the texts of a worthy religion at last, one which we may wholeheartedly admire, in part because we are not required to believe in it or pay it tithes.

Doctor Serafico, the princess von Thurn und Taxis-Hohenlohe called him. More appropriately, Doctor Dodge . . . Doctor Ricochet . . . as we follow this summary full of repetitions of repetition:

In Linz, it is Olga, in Prague, it is Vally who helps him publish; then Rilke meets Lou, his lover/mother, in Munich, follows her to Berlin, accompanies her to Danzig, St. Petersburg, and back to Berlin again; he vacations in Viareggio, where he meets Elena; enjoys the company of Paula and Clara at Worpswede; marries Clara when bounced by Lou, although he does so against Lou's good advice, and rolls to Westerwede, where there is a charming little cottage soon too full of child cries and other obnoxious duties; consequently he's shortly off to Paris, where Rodin (and not a woman) is the lure, but it is no fun being poor in Paris, even if the parks are pretty; so with Clara (who has parked the kid with her parents), Rilke escapes to Rome, then volleys north to visit Ellen Key in Scandinavia, where he's handsomely taken care of by her friends, until it is time to return to Bremen, Göttingen (one of Lou Salomé's haunts), and Berlin again; but not for long, because it's Rilke's luck to enjoy a few more elegant estates—the Countess von Schwerin's, the Baron von der Heydt's, the beginning of a pleasant habit—before trudging back to Paris and a crankier Rodin.

Such summations are forms of exaggeration, yet so are maps and travel tables and those figures in the carpet.

It is a life of packing and unpacking, of smiling at new friends, looking out of different windows, sitting in trains, trying to write at odd and irregular hours, signing books and behaving like a literary lion, having ideas, getting used to strange dark halls, guest beds, always cadging and scrounging, eating poorly, keeping your pants pressed, and most of all, falling ill, the flu a favorite, sneezing into a pillow, dozing while wrapped up in a chair: life time which gets little report, for what is there to say about a sore throat or a coughing fit? the fumble to find a chamber pot beneath strangely squeaking springs? a scheme to put one's ear out of range of the sleep-inducing bore who's been seated at your left?

It is a life of loneliness, of brooding, self-absorption, moods the world seems to mirror, because all the hours most of us spend making a living in office or schoolroom or farm or factory, Rilke has on his hands. Hence all those letters, of course, a prodigious output of prose, prose which rehearsed his life so it might play as a poem.

The leaves are falling, falling from far away,
as though a distant garden died above us;
they fall, fall with denial in their wave.

And through the night the hard earth falls
farther than the stars in solitude.

We all are falling. Here, this hand falls.
And see—there goes another. It's in us all.

And yet there's One whose gently holding hands
let this falling fall and never land.[14]

Later in that same September of 1902, he feels autumn on him
once again.

Lord, it is time. The summer was too long.
Lay your shadow on the sundials now,
and through the meadows let the winds throng.

Ask the last fruits to ripen on the vine;
give them further two more summer days
to bring about perfection and to raise
the final sweetness in the heavy wine.

Whoever has no house now will establish none,
whoever lives alone now will live on long alone,
will waken, read, and write long letters,
wander up and down the barren paths
the parks expose when leaves are blown.[15]

It is a life of taking in: landscapes and atmospheres, both run-
down rooms and lush islands, portrait galleries in this *Schloss*

and that lodge, books by forgotten Scandinavians, but sometimes by equals like Valéry, Flaubert, or Proust, paintings by Cézanne, sculpture by Rodin: training his eye not to flinch, to see the thing seen and not to be the wadded ball of feeling his young heart flung at things; to absorb sensation as if it were food, and live on its sustenance, even in hibernation. *Regarde!* The result of his labor is to be found in the merciless exactness of *Malte Laurids Brigge*: "At last I am learning to see."

Most important, Rilke's life is the life of a great writer, a poet who trained on prose, who made his weaknesses into warriors. It is therefore a life which is built of those great moments when, at white heat, he creates whole populations of poems and stories: the entire *Book of Monkish Life* from September 20 to October 14 in 1899, followed by *The Stories of God* from November 10 to 21; then thirty poems of *The Book of Pilgrimage* from September 18 to 25 in 1901, the thirty-four poems of *The Book of Hours* from April 13 to 20 in 1903, the stanzas which make up *The Life of Mary* between January 15 and 22 of 1912, the sudden announcement in Duino of the *Elegies* on the same month's 21st, or, of course, the greatest inspirational storm, perhaps, in poetry's history, the *Elegies'* surprising completion in Muzot when, as if a tap had been left running, a sequence of sonnets he would dedicate to Orpheus appeared in the space of three days, from February 2 to 5 in 1922, priming the pump, as it were, to draw forth "The Sixth Elegy," compose the "Seventh," then the "Eighth" and "Ninth," as his pen entered the second week of that sacred month, with the main body of the "Tenth" to arrive on the 11th like a flourish of trumpets. The cycle is not complete just yet. A "Fifth Elegy" is replaced by another on the 14th. The hinge of the set is the last one written, perhaps the most bitter elegy of all, a bitterness which sounds in the final notes of his triumph.

These explosions of poetry were regularly accompanied by

prose—such was the pattern of the past—and it was no different this time: Rilke writes *The Young Workman's Letter*, summing up his attitudes toward art, Christianity, and sexuality, in his most important prose piece since *The Notebooks of Malte Laurids Brigge*. As if he is hitched to a runaway, the second section of the *Sonnets to Orpheus* rushes into being in eight more February days. There are now fifty-five of these dense yet crystalline poems. And Rilke still has the energy to write numerous triumphant letters. What had been wrung from him was more than wine.

It caps a life, and Rilke feels, in a way, that he has been concluded like a symphony. Yet, as Edward Snow points out in *Uncollected Poems, Rainer Maria Rilke*,[16] his alleged dry spells, his troughs, are dotted, as a dry creek by nuggets, with remarkable poems (as occasional as lit matches in a crowd) which Rilke simply does not bother to collect, his focus elsewhere, or his health a painful preoccupation.

Raum. If there were one word it would be *Raum.* The space of things. The space of outer space. The space of night which comes through porous windows to feed on our faces. The mystical carpet where lovers wrestle. The womb of the mother. *Weltraum.* Not just the room in which the furniture of the world rests, but the space of the things themselves. The space made by Being's breathing. Then *Innerweltraum.* (The German language, the German spirit, can and must compound.) Not just the space we call consciousness, but the space where we retire in order to avoid a feeling, the touch of a lover, the plea of a friend, the threat of intimacy. Distance. Darkness dotted by stars. These spaces are always palpable, as though space were smoke, or the mountains of the heart where the last hamlet of feeling may be discerned. The various distances of death. Time itself is a spaceline. For when we are dead we journey on through what we once believed was past. Cathedral spaces. The spaces made by music. *Innerweltraum*. The slopes shaped by the word in the countrysides of poetry.

Music: breathing of statues. Possibly:
stillness in pictures. Speech where speech
ends. Time upright and poised
upon the coastline of our passions.

Feelings for whom? You are the transformation
of all feeling into—what? . . . audible landscape.
You stranger: music. Heart's space
that's outgrown us. Innermost us
which it's scaled, surmounted, gone beyond
into holiest absence:
where what's within surrounds us
the way the most skillful horizon does,
or the other side of the air,
pure,
immense,
no longer lived in.[17]

Similarly, *The Notebooks of Malte Laurids Brigge* are not to be moved through like so many passing minutes. Isn't any book of hours, because it is a book, a thing? and if it is a thing, it is a space—two spaces, really, the space it makes and the space it's in—and if it is a space, it exists all at once, not bit by bit or leaf by leaf or line by line. The scenes in the novel which fasten the two notebooks together depict the famous unicorn tapestries in Paris' Cluny Museum. And the whole of *Malte* is built, is painted, is woven, like those calm and gracious images, symbols for each of the senses. They are there all at once, traveled over by the eye, made of threads, but they are not thin, lengthy, or

line-like like threads, these flowered places where solemn creatures hover like symbols hung about a hidden neck.

Every line which Rainer Maria Rilke wrote in early life is
there in later life: an *Offering to the Lares* and the *Sonnets to
Orpheus* may stand beside one another like two parked bikes,
and I in fact did read the so-called later poems before I read
their many predecessors. So the poet's development is drawn
now on a lifemap held flat on a tabletop. I may, if I wish, travel
back or go forth or leap ahead—into books in which Rilke is
only subject matter—where words about him are the only
words.

Everything passes, there is nowhere we can rest, even if it is
on a flight to Egypt; yet what did Proust prove? That the world
can be taken out of time and given a place. A place in perma-
nence. Because *rühmen dass ist*. The most modest object—a bit
of lace, perhaps—can provide proof.

And if one day all we do and suffer done
should seem suddenly trivial and strange,
as though it were no longer clear
why we should have kicked off our childhood shoes
for such things—would not this length
of yellowed lace, this densely woven swatch
of linen flowers, be enough to hold us here?
See: this much was accomplished.

A life, perhaps, was made too little of, who knows?
a happiness in hand let slip; yet despite this,
for each loss there appeared in its place
this spun-out thing, no lighter than life,
and yet perfect, and so beautiful that all our so-be-its
are no longer too early, smiled at, and held in abeyance.[18]

This much was accomplished. But when Rilke reached Paris on August 28, 1902, to study and write on Rodin, he was still a young man in his twenties, given to depressions and hysterical highs, to enthusiasms which overmatched their causes, and to the habit of seeking in the world convenient containers for his copious but volatile and uneducated feelings. He needed to be reformed and focused, and he was: by Paris, by the example of Rodin, by the poetry of Baudelaire, which so suited its site and Rilke's moods, by the fictions of Flaubert, and maybe most of all by the paintings of Cézanne.

Not the dots but the distance between them that creates the line; not the lines which turn into contours, but the planes between; not simply the planes but the surfaces they define; not the surfaces alone but the light with which they combine to bring every point upon them vibrantly to life: these were some of the things he learned. He learned that in one's art an elbow may flow into a thigh, a chin disappear into a palm, a walker walk more purely without the distraction of arms; he learned how a figure might emerge from a chunk of marble like a plant from the ground; he learned that "there are tears which pour from all pores" because everything has an expression, a face where a smile alone lives; that there is stone that can be set in motion, or a motion held like a pose; that every accident should be made necessary, and every necessity look like a towel thrown over the back of a chair—these were a few of the lessons he took to heart: that the poet's eye needs to be so candid that even a decaying vulva, full of flies, must be fearlessly reported, following Baudelaire's example; that exactitude is prerequisite to achievement, so that whatever is full should be fully shown, but rendered spare when sparse, and empty when empty; above all, that art is actually the opposite of nature, and that the creation of being—the breathing of statues—is what counts; not the imitation of nature but its transformation is the artist's aim: these were some of the things he learned, they began his *Wendung*, his moment of "turning." Finally, Rilke learned what seeing is, and then he learned to see.

"To see" means to taste and thereby to "dance the orange," to touch and feel at one's finger end a little eternity, to smell our-selves cloud like steam from a warm cup, to hear voices, to lis-ten so intensely you rise straight from the ground.

And he saw a man growing from the shoulder of a seated woman; he saw Orpheus—Eurydice behind him helpless—Orpheus' hand at his eyes; he saw a sculpture called *The Death of the Poet*, another called *The Prodigal Son*; he saw plaster cou-ples intertwined; he saw sleeping marbles, and birds of stone so artfully wrought that every feather implied flight and therefore a sky to fly through; he saw a victim of St. Vitus' dance jiggling and convulsing on a Paris street, blind men blind and beggars begging; he saw a woman who, in grief, left her face in her hands: each called forth poems . . . eventually . . . prose that equaled the best of his poems . . . poems that filled space as much as their subjects did, such as the Buddha he contem-plated so often in Rodin's garden at Meudon.

> As if he listened. Silence. Depth.
> And we hold back our breath. Yet nothing yet.
> And he is star. And other great stars ring him,
> though we cannot see that far.
>
> O he is fat. Do we suppose
> he'll see us? He has need of that?
> Sink in any supplicating pose before him,
> he'll sit deep and idle as a cat.
>
> For that which lures us to his feet
> has circled in him now a million years.

He has forgotten all we must endure,
encloses all we would escape.[19]

Rodin had an actual exhibition pavilion from the 1900 Paris World's Fair moved to his property in Meudon-Val-Fleury, just outside the city. In this building, which was flanked by Rodin's own manor house and surrounded by a number of cottages, workshops, studios, he installed a bounty of his sculptures. On the grounds were placed numerous stone pieces, both whole and in fragments, both Rodin's own and antique, including the Buddha just celebrated. Among the statuary minced many doves, in spite of the dogs, and on the grounds near the banks of the river three swans managed to waddle. Here, too, the *New Poems* emerged, the *Dinggedicht*—a set of solids set in their book as if in a gallery. As Norbert Fuerst correctly observes: "It is characteristic of many of these chiseled and sculptured poems that one can read them backwards, or that one can read back and forth in them. They are more spatial than temporal."[20]

Eventually, and for a time, enlisted as Rodin's secretary, Rilke will occupy a cottage at Meudon, lunch with Rodin and his anxious wifewishing mistress, feed the swans, and inspect the stones.

I wonder if Rilke ever realized how ironic the outcome of his and Rodin's careers would be, for Rilke leaves the Master to become a Master, to grow through each succeeding year toward his whirlwind, while Rodin is sucked by sycophants into a whirlpool. Sexually overcome . . . again and again . . . Rodin is tamed by an American lady who has managed with Jamesian ingenuity to become a duchess. She dressed him, Kenneth Clark says, "in a silk top-hat and frock coat and led him round Europe in a black limousine like a dancing bear." When Rodin finally got rid of her (beseeched to do so by friends), he remained at Meudon, where the parasites could find him and deprive him of his intestines. "The chorus of praise from enthusiastic ladies and *littérateurs*," in Clark's opinion, "was calculated to bring out the worst in his genius for it dwelt on the pseudo-mystic qualities in his work."[21] That is precisely what many of Rilke's female friends offered him: adoration of his flaws. But they only induced in him a weakness for séances and table-tipping. One must fly from fan and foe alike, for how alike they are. Saved because sex could not entrap him; saved because he always needed . . .

Raum. And felt the fear of its lack. Breathing room. He walks the parks, but even when crowded, the parks are vacant, because the spiritual spaces between the people who form the crowds are empty. The poet has sought solitude and found only loneliness. At the zoo, the animals appear superior, yet even they pace, turn like the horses of the carousel, or like the panther in that celebrated poem:

> His gaze has grown so worn from the passing
> of the bars that it sees nothing anymore.
> There seem to be a thousand bars before him
> and beyond that thousand nothing of the world.
>
> The supple motion of his panther's stride,
> as he pads through a tightening circle,
> is like the dance of strength around a point
> on which an equal will stands stupefied.
>
> Only rarely is an opening in the eyes
> enabled. Then an image brims
> which slides the quiet tension of the limbs
> until the heart, wherein it dies.[22]

Rilke's strategy for the defeat of time was to turn it into space. In that way what was passing—and everything was—merely passed on to another part of reality. Sometimes, if it were the water of a fountain, its changing never changed. And the observer's inner world would be spread out inside him like an alpine meadow or even an armed camp or an independent country, despite the fact that consciousness has no objective location. Emotions could be measured and sited among the mountains of the heart, so when love died, it died of closeness and confinement, not from aging or duration.

> Aren't lovers
> always arriving at the borders of each other,
> although both promised breathing space, unimpeded
>   hunting, home?[23]

But habits die hard; nothing utterly passes. Life patterns see to it that actions, attitudes, conditions, return—the painter, Baladine Klossowska, is replaced by the poet, Marina Tsvetaeva, for instance, and Rilke's early connection with Russia reappears when Marina's first letter arrives. His name, she said, was a poem in itself. That was a good start to an epistolary love affair similar to all the others except in acceleration. Marina drew him out and on. Into another elegy, one he named for her. How could she know that this was not a good omen?

It was not time which did him in, for he had years ahead of him. It was not the women, for he eluded them. It was leukemia, the cancer that kills children, the cancer that claimed his daughter's playmate Wera Knoop; an illness of the blood we know now is most often borne by our genes, and is therefore the death sent by our ancestors: the ragged core of a sweet apple to erupt—sore and swollen—in the poet's mouth. It was indeed Rilke's proper death (if there is any that's proper), running like fire through his veins, just as he had written, ostensibly address-ing God, "and if you set this mind of mine aflame, then on my blood I'll carry you away."

Refusing narcotics in order to keep a clear head, the better to confront his illness, Rilke wrote letters to friends describing his agony, a few lines of verse too, no longer French, inscribed on flyleafs. He also composed his testament in which he begged his intimates, should his faculties be dimmed, to prevent any priestly intervention when his soul "moved into the open."

Symbolic hopes were held out against his sickness like talis-mans. A three-hundred-year-old goat willow, planted in the courtyard of the von Salis castle because the willow's Latin name was *Salix caprea*, and hence a suitable emblem for the family, had miraculously restored itself by driving a new root down through its rotten trunk from an upper branch; and Rilke copied "The Willow of Salenegg" into the guest book of that house. Could he reroot too? That was in August. He would die at the year's end. But his thought then would be of the pain that was passing like a filament through all the other aches and angers of his life. Rilke admonishes us not to confuse the ill-nesses of childhood, for instance, which were respites, even subterfuges, with those of dying. In a little notebook, he wrote his final lines:

> Come on in now, you last of the pains I will admit,
> incurable, into my body's web.
> As my spirit burns—see—I burn
> in you; the wood no longer can deny
> its agreement with the flame you're flaming.
> You burn me, but I inside your burning burn.
>
> My present mildness, in your ferocity, will be
> not of here but there, most hellishly.

I climbed this pyre, faggots piled to fearful heights,
convinced I'd never sacrifice
my soul's uncounted sum to gain a future.
Am I still he who—unacknowledged—burns here?
I'll not call my memories to burn nearby me.
O life—outside me—Oh to live you.
And I aflame. Known now to none.[24]

TRANSREADING

In a translation, one language, and one particular user of that language, reads another.

> Mit gelben Birnen hänget
> Und voll mit wilden Rosen
> Das Land in den See,

If I am reading Friedrich Hölderlin's German in German, the language will be trying to understand itself. Out of the number of words which German offers, Hölderlin has chosen these, and I can let them ring in my head as if heard. "With yellow pears hangs / And full with wild roses / the land in the lake." Easily said, less easily understood, because the order of the words is—well—wild as the roses are.

These lines, first of all, send me to experience. I remember how, when heavily fruited, the fruit tree's branches are bowed; and I remember how, in the clear fall light, flowers, bushes, trees are oddly reflected in still water as if actually upside down, and directly beneath themselves, an optically odd apparition. Then I may read the poem's title ("Hälfte des Lebens") again, and realize that the pears and their image are halves of one real, unreal whole.

The land, heavy with fruit and flowers, hangs down into the

lake, where object and reflection are joined. I ask myself why the natural order is interrupted. Shouldn't it be: "With yellow pears, and full of wild roses, the land hangs down into the lake"? But then the word *hänget* wouldn't hang.

Every line of fine literature forms a secure, seemingly serene, yet unquiet community. As in any community, there are many special interests and the groups which promote them; there are predominating concerns, persistent problems; and, as in the psyche of any individual, or in the larger region of the body politic, there are competing aims, anxieties, habits, anticipations, perplexities, memories, needs, and grievances. When the line is a good one, their clamor is stilled because its constituents are happy, their wants appeased, their aims fulfilled.

When the line is a good one, there is a musical movement to its meaning which binds the line together as if it were one word, yet at the same time articulating, weighing, and apportioning the line's particular parts the way syllables and their sounds and stresses spell a noun or verb, while throwing down a pattern of rhythm and meaning like a path to be pursued deeper into the stanza, and resonating with what has preceded it, if anything has. These are not naturally harmonious functions: looking forward, listening back, uniting and differentiating.

Half of life has been lived. Heavy with its succulent fruit, that life looks down upon its future, but it is a future in which this present, now past, can only be remembered. The reflection in the water resembles reality almost exactly, yet it is just that—a picture. And you and I then, adopting the poet's position, can halve ourselves to see what we are now as well as what we shall become: illusory.

What a beautiful idea: earth, solid and settled, flesh rosy and trim, life full and accomplished, altering into water, into remembrance, into image.

Ihr holden Schwäne,
Und trunken von Küssen
Tunkt ihr das Haupt
Ins heilignüchterne Wasser.

Upon this water swans are swimming so calmly the reflection of
the land they float upon is undisturbed. "You lovely swans, and
drunk from kisses you dip your heads into the holy sobering
water." There is another interruption of the normal order here
which exactly parallels the first ("and full with wild roses"). It is
the habit of swans to do a bit of necking, and bill dipping too.
This information comes to us from some swan watching. That
the swan (most notable for its raucous, peacock-like scream) is
supposed to sing a sweetly accepting song at the point of death
is handed down to us from myth.

It is likely that English speakers will have already read Yeats'
"The Wild Swans at Coole," which opens upon a similar landscape and at the same time of year.

The trees are in their autumn beauty,
The woodland paths are dry,
Under the October twilight the water
Mirrors a still sky;
Upon the brimming water among the stones
Are nine-and-fifty swans.

And there is no reason at all why we should have to forget, reading Hölderlin, everything we know that came after him. As
Borges has taught us, all the books in the library are contemporary. Great poems are like granaries: they are always ready to
enlarge their store.

Rilke's extraordinary Leda poem will get written later, as well as his charming though more modest lyric titled simply "The Swan."

> We struggle through the undone and the yet-to-do
> as though our legs were shackled, hobbling on and on
> with the awkward waddle of the swan.
>
> And dying—to lose our footing on the ground
> we daily counted on to hold us—
> is like the anxious swan's surrender

> to the water which receives him with all honor,
> drawing aside like a curtain in the wind,
> receding wave on wave to shape his wake,
> while he, stately, still, remote, assured,
> majestically indifferent and composed,
> condescends to glide.[1]

In the *Elegies* Rilke won't find death likely to offer such easy sailing. There will be much undoing to get done, much past life to leave.

Hölderlin's swan, sailing between earth and water, its own image riding beside it, and drunk with the kisses which convey the primeness of life, sobers itself by sipping from the cup of consequence: that the first half of one's history will linger on in the second half only in recollection.

Translating is reading, reading of the best, the most essential, kind. The adjective "gracious" barely hides what the German is franker about—the poem's religious allusions—for the swans are dipping their heads *ins heilignüchterne Wasser*. That *heilignüchterne* is one helluva word. Christopher Middleton, in his fine version, says "you gracious swans" and then ends "into the holy lucid water," while Michael Hamburger, in his equally excellent try, writes "you lovely swans" to close with "into the hallowed, the sober water." "Gracious," unfortunately, doesn't mean "graceful," and "graceful" doesn't mean "full of grace" anymore. But if the swans are lovely (as I'm certain they are), they're only lovely, which isn't enough. The cool fall water will have a sobering effect, to be sure, but I'm not convinced it should be like a splash in the face. I don't dare do "holy sober" either. There's no place for that kind of pun in this poem. So I'm going to take a chance and push the religious undertones up a little. And I have to remember to hold off on hanging the land.

> With yellow pears, the land,
> and full of wild roses,
> hangs down into the lake.
> You graceshaped swans,
> drunk from kisses,
> you dip your heads
> into the holy solemn water.

The swans are graceful and lovely, and the water is lucid and sobering and solemn, hallowed and holy. In this case, one does not "opt," but one must choose.[2]

It's been frequently said that translation is a form of betrayal: it is a traduction, a reconstitution made of sacrifice and revision. One bails to keep the boat afloat. However, we don't have to give up everything. Neither swans themselves, nor their symbolic significance, is uniquely German. We won't have to replace them. The season and its meaning, the reflective power of a pond: these things are easily retained. The central ideas of the stanza, provided we have a proper hold on them, can be transported without loss. When the poem asks a question, we can ask one; when it asserts or describes or avows, we can follow. The general shape of the sonnet can be repeated too, but the poem does not want to be squeezed into its form like an ill-fitting suit; it hopes to flower forth in fourteen lines as if all its genes said, "Bloom." The sonnet shape is as powerful as a right-wing religious group, however, conservative to the core, and snooty to boot. The meter wants to march five abreast across the page, arm swinging smartly up to strike the chest, eyes must move right at the right time; rhyme waits like a tympanist, sticks poised above the paper and the tightened lines it would make resonate; alliteration wants to twist the tongue as much as asso-nance would soothe it; there is the short word which sounds long, like "oboe," and the thin tight-lipped ones like "pit," to be played against those of generously open ends like "oboe" again, and of course, "Ohio," as well as words long in print but short of sound, or hissies such as "Mississippi," lovely liquids like "hal-lelujah," and undulating beauties such as "Alabama."

Moreover, the right sorts of sacrifice are essential. We had better lose the poem's German sounds and German order, because we are trying to achieve the poem Hölderlin would have written had he been English. We can't make it move too smoothly and go whistling along. Here is my version of its clos-ing seven:

> Where shall I, when
> winter's here, find flowers,
> and where sunshine
> and shadows of earth?
> Walls stand speechless
> and cold, in the wind
> weathercocks clatter.

Middleton has "weathervane," but I must follow Hamburger here, not only for a better sound, but because I want to call qui-etly for the cock who discomfited Peter. The German con cludes *Klirren die Fahnen*, and could be interpreted as "flags flap," but nationalism has not had any presence in the preceding lines.

What we get when we're done is a reading, a reading enriched by the process of arriving at it, and therefore, really, only the farewells to a long conversation.

What must not be given up, of course, is quality—quality and tone. If the translation does not allow us a glimpse of the greatness of the original, it is surely a failure, and most of us fail that way, first and foremost, last and out of luck. Tone, too, is a very tricky thing. Recently Anita Barrows and Joanna Macy translated Rilke's *Book of Hours* for Riverhead Books. Here is a sample. The poet is presumably addressing his god, but we know the divinity in question is actually Rilke's quondam lover, Lou Salomé.

> Extinguish my eyes, I'll go on seeing you.
> Seal my ears, I'll go on hearing you.
> And without feet I can make my way to you,
> without a mouth I can swear your name.
>
> Break off my arms, I'll take hold of you
> with my heart as with a hand.
> Stop my heart, and my brain will start to beat.
> And if you consume my brain with fire,
> I'll feel you burn in every drop of my blood.[3]

I feel that the tone of my version is fiercer, more ardent, but it is perhaps more a love poem now than a religious one.

> Put my eyes out: I can still see;
> slam my ears shut: I can still hear,
> walk without feet to where you were,

and, tongueless, speak you into being.
Snap off my arms: I'll hold you hard
in my heart's longing like a fist;
halt that, my brain will do its beating,
and if you set this mind of mine aflame,
then on my blood I'll carry you away.[4]

It will usually take many readings to arrive at the right place. Somewhere amid various versions like a ghost the original will drift. Yet our situation is no different if we are trying to understand English with English eyes. Hardy begins his great poem about love rendered-as-rhyme with this nine-liner:

> If it's ever Spring again,
>   Spring again,
> I shall go where went I when
> Down the moor-cock splashed, and hen,
> Seeing me not, amid their flounder,
> Standing with my arms around her;
> If it's ever Spring again,
>   Spring again,
> I shall go where went I then.

Try "translating" Hardy's English into your own. "I shall go where I once saw the moor-cock and his mate splash down, locked in one another's wings. I notice them but they do not see me standing nearby with my arms around my own beloved." I must not omit the awkward beauty of the refrain, "I shall go where went I when," and any change I make will reinforce the rightness of the original. If I lose the rhymes, I lose the poem, for there are four in a row before the couplet, and then three more returns of the initial sound. There is a reason for this rhyme scheme which Hardy subsequently reveals.

If it's ever summer-time,
    Summer-time,
With the hay crop at the prime,
And the cuckoos—two—in rhyme,
As they used to be, or seemed to,
We shall do as long we've dreamed to,
If it's ever summer-time,
    Summer-time,
With the hay, and bees achime.

To read with recognition (not just simple understanding) is to realize why the writer made the choices he or she made, and why, if the writing has been done well (suppose I'd said "well done"?), its words could not have been set down otherwise. Our translations will make a batch of botches, but it will not matter, crush them all into a ball and toss them to the trash. Their real value will have been received. The translating reader reads the inside of the verse and sees, like the physician, either its evident health or its hidden disease. That reader will know why Hardy couldn't come right out and say: "Someday we'll have a roll in the hay."

EIN GOTT VERMAGS

What lover of poetry has not read the story? Rainer Maria Rilke, that rootless poet whom we've followed like a stray for so long we know the smell of his heels, has been lent the off-season use of the Castle Duino by the Princess Marie von Thurn und Taxis-Hohenlohe. The place is huge and stern, alternately menacing and boring, too austere even for a soul sold on austerity. Rilke, as sensitive to weather as a vane, also found the climate trying. Yet it was economical. It spoke to him only of work. Nevertheless, the poet would have preferred Capri. Duino it was.

Pent up there by a bitter Adriatic winter and, more willingly, by the stones of the place itself, he continues to be deserted by his Muse so that he feels barren, arid of spirit, yet driven deeply into himself like a stake meant for his own heart. Sterile as a wooden cuckoo, then, and surrounded like the sea below him by a loneliness which has for months embarrassed his much prized solitude with occult visitations and handmade sex, shaming and humiliating him, the Poet has had—this fateful morning—to deal with an annoying business letter he feels asks too loudly for its answer. Preoccupied, he walks along the precipitous edge of the Duino Castle cliffs, his head bent into a bright wind which buries his breath. Then . . . then, like the rattle in a hollow gourd, he hears in his head what will one day be the cel-

56

ebrated question with which the *Elegies* are at last to announce themselves: *Wer, wenn ich schriee, hörte mich denn aus der Engel Ordnungen?*

Or (in the presence of any poet is it possible to say the phrase?)—in other words:

Leishman. (1939/60) Who, if I cried, would hear me among the angelic orders?

Behn. (1957) Who, if I cried out, would heed me amid the host of the Angels?

MacIntyre. (1961) Who, if I shouted, among the hierarchy of angels would hear me?

Garmey/Wilson. (1972) Who, if I cried, would hear me from the order of Angels?

Boney. (1975) Who of the angelic hosts would hear me, even if I cried out?

Poulin. (1977) And if I cried, who'd listen to me in those angelic orders?

Young. (1978) If I cried out
    who would hear me up there
      among the angelic orders?

Miranda. (1981) What angel, if I cried out, would hear me?

Mitchell. (1982) Who, if I cried out, would hear me among the angels' hierarchies?

Flemming. (1985) Who, if I cried out, would hear me among the angels' hierarchies?

Hunter. (1987) Who, though I cry aloud, would hear me in the angel order?

Cohn. (1989) WHO, if I cried out, might hear me— among the ranked Angels?

Hammer/Jaeger. (1991) If I did cry out, who would hear me through the Angel Orders?

Oswald. (1992)   Who, if I cried out, would hear me
then, out of the orders of angels?

Gass. (1998)   Who, if I cried, would hear me among
the Dominions of Angels?

In so many other words . . .

When, in 1975, Ingo Seidler presented his "Critical Appraisal of English Versions of Rilke" to a Rilke Centennial at Wayne State University,[1] he remarked on "the astonishing bulk of available English versions" of Rilke's work in print, at least according to publishers' catalogues. "Five complete translations of the *Duino Elegies* are listed" (Leishman to Boney, in my enumeration), and Professor Seidler says he knows "of at least another two." What must he think now when my catalogue (surely not exhaustive) finds without trying fourteen complete versions as well as many incomplete ones? Nor of course are the *Elegies* the sole target of the translators, who have given us new renderings of Rilke's fiction (both novels and stories), his published poetry, his uncollected poems, his early plays, his journals, his ventures into French verse, as well as many of his countless letters.

If I receive some petty request in the post (can't we imagine our poet peevishly complaining as he picks his way down the narrow path to the bastions?), even a nag from a nobody, good manners compel me to respond; its silliness will occupy my thoughts like a game of cards; but if I were to entreat the higher powers, cry out from my soul, pray to the so-called gods for my poetry to be returned to me, for a little rain after this long drought, whom would my words reach?

No one. The mountains of the heart entertain no echo. The Abyss does not respond. Heaven is as indifferent as the land. The ocean holds no intermission.

But the voice, of course, is not heard as the poet's own. It comes from the clean wind, the bora, burning his face like the sun, and it has the same elemental force, the same cold grip, as the streaming air which would lift him like a leaf and whirl him away over the glare of the sea.

Thus it is not the fastidious, fussy little person of the petitioner who wonders these words (it is everybody's elemental outcry); and although addressed to the Angels, it is as if the Angels spoke them, because their meaning is not common, small, or mean—earthbound—as most of our fears and worries are, most of our thoughts, hopelessly human as we are; hence the poem which appears like the wind in our ear must have all the fundamental mystery and breathtaking grandeur we feel whenever we encounter that simple, plain, and pure correctness about the nature of things which only the gods possess.

These are not poems, then. These are miracles. And they must seem miraculous . . . *Ein Gott vermags.*

Well, can we make up our minds? does the poet cry or shout or, again, cry out? aloud? and do the angels fail to hear or heed or listen to him? How deep is their indifference? The cry is surely an inward cry, a cry to heaven as empty as the air, a cry blown out like a flame. Why write "cry out" then? . . . to avoid any sense of sniveling. Yet this cry, in a few lines, will include the child's. In any case, it is scarcely so crude as a shout. And the Angels, more self-absorbed than Narcissus, will not hear, let alone listen, not to say heed. Nor are they l.c. angels, smallish, cupid-like. They surpass Gabriel, who has to fetch, toot, and carry. What then does this dissonant clamor from the tents of the translators come to?

My version has striven for a more euphonious line and has tried to reflect the hierarchy which *Ordnungen* suggests by invoking one of the arrangements associated with the traditional conception of angels, namely their division into seraphim, cherubim, thrones—dominations, virtues, powers—principalities, archangels, angels; but Behn's and Boney's "hosts" are entirely too churchy, while MacIntyre's "shout" and again Behn's "heed" are simply misinterpretations.

As for that preposition: is it to be "among the Angelic orders," "amid" them, "from" them, or "in" or "out" instead? Hammer/Jaeger's "through" is simply bizarre. Poulin wants the angels not only to "hear" but to "listen," while Behn requires obedience. The nature of Rilke's Angels is such, as the *Elegies* will indicate as they proceed, that although they might find themselves in an order, they would never arrange it, no more than the stars might design their constellations. The hierarchy isn't theirs, even if Mitchell and Flemming would have it so. Boney and Miranda want to single out an angel like a calf from the herd, while Hunter and Hammer/Jaeger bump "order" and "Angel" awkwardly together. Cohn's expression "ranked Angels" sounds ludicrous in English (Angel A, Angel B . . .).

No one has tried to mimic the *wenn-denn* division—a discretion which was no doubt wise, though Oswald puts in one of them while incidentally doubling his "out" ("Who, if I cried out, would hear me then, out of the orders of angels?"). Poulin's rendering is oddest of all, because the initial "And" implies a prior speech, an earlier communication, although nothing, surely, is prior to the poet's profound recognition of his isolation. In addition, Poulin is far too colloquial for the *Elegies* ("who'd listen to me" has totally the wrong tone), but Young is even worse ("who would hear me up there"). These are not the sounds we should hear if our voice were to echo from the edges of the distant gods and were thus to return to us as a primitive original the way a deeply dappled shadow might replace—might cast back—its tree.

The *Elegies* are dominated by Angels of an icy sky above and the gravitating dactyls of a declining ground below, with the dactyls by far the more powerful presence. When, as in the opening question, that meter is easy to maintain, it should be as thankfully embraced as an accommodating woman. And when the word order, so often a twisting and rocky road, is also straightforward, why not be straightforward? The *Elegies* tell us to listen as hitherto only holy men have listened. The individuality, the quirkiness, the bone-headed nature of every translation is inevitable. I see no reason to strive for these qualities.

All in all, then, Leishman must be accounted the most adequate, and perhaps even the only acceptable, version: he has roughly the right meter (unlike Poulin or Young, for instance); he keeps the same sequence of words (unlike MacIntyre, Boney, Poulin, Miranda, and Hammer/Jaeger), especially retaining the Germanic *Engel Ordnungen;* he maintains the proper tone (unlike MacIntyre, Poulin, and Young); he has the correct interpretation (unlike Behm, Poulin, Miranda, Hammer/Jaeger, and Oswald); even if one might reasonably complain that "angelic" in English carries too many inappropriate connotations. Although Poulin gets generally bad marks, and Young and Hammer/Jaeger are pretty awful, MacIntyre's "shout" seems to me to be the most jarring mistake.

Now we reach that "and" which Poulin was in such an unseemly hurry to get in: *und gesetzt seibst, es nähme einer mich plützlich ans Herz: ich verginge von seinem stärkeren Dasein.*

Leishman.   And even if one of them suddenly pressed me
             against his heart, I should fade in the strength
             of his stronger existence.

Behn.   Still, should an Angel exalt and fold me into
             his heart I should vanish, lost in his greater
             being.

MacIntyre.	And supposing one of them took me suddenly to his heart, I would perish before his stronger existence.
Garmey/Wilson.	And even if one suddenly held me to his heart: I would dissolve there from his stronger presence.
Boney.	Yet granted, one of them suddenly embraced me, I would only perish from his stronger being.
Poulin.	Even if one of them suddenly held me to his heart, I'd vanish in his overwhelming presence.

Young.

> And suppose one suddenly
>> took me to his heart
>>> I would shrivel
>
> I couldn't survive
>> next to his
>>> greater existence.

Miranda.	And even if one of them impulsively embraced me, I'd be crushed by its strength.
Mitchell.	and even if one of them pressed me suddenly against his heart: I would be consumed in that overwhelming existence.
Flemming.	and even if one of them suddenly pressed me against his heart, I would perish in the embrace of his stronger existence.

Hunter.

> And should my plea ascend,
> were I gathered to the glory
> of some incandescent heart,
> my own faint flame of being
> would fail for the glare.

Cohn.	Even if One suddenly clasped me to his heart I would die of the force of his being.

Hammer/Jaeger.	and suppose one of them suddenly pulled me to his heart: I'd dissolve beside his stronger existence.
Oswald.	and even supposing one suddenly took me close to the heart, I would perish from that stronger existence.
Gass.	And even if one of them suddenly held me against his heart, I would fade in the grip of that completer existence.

The strength of the Angels is not the strength of Hercules, who could lift even Antaeus from the earth (although we are offered a wrestler's image), but consists in the louder *da* of a superior *Dasein*. The Angels are what the poet would be if he could free himself from human distraction, if he could be indifferent to the point of divinity, absorbed in himself like all noumena are, and at one with the work and the world of the work, its radiant perfections, like those twice luminous worms which glow with the added glory of their own phosphorescence: the lower light flouncing outward like a shout, the higher—that rare instreaming Rilkean light— swirling toward its source like water softly down a drain. Thus the friendliest hug of these Angels would be more than anyone could bear.

Most of the hands here hold the right cards, but few know how to play them. Leishman, otherwise excellent, reflecting the sibilance of the German, has the poet "fade in the strength," the wrong preposition for this phrase, though the clearly right one for the wrapped-within sense of the original. Behn tries "fold," perhaps for that reason. Nevertheless, Leishman's image is too wrestlerish. The other temptation is to be too amorous about the embrace. The Angel is not out to crush us, as Miranda has it, nor is he seeking a confidant, as Oswald and MacIntyre intimate ("took me close to the heart," "took me suddenly to his heart"), nor is he showing, by this gesture, some emotional warmth, which a word like "embrace" suggests. Behn's "exalt" comes out of nowhere.

Why the heart? To hear it beat, one presumes, to feel the power of the Angel's actuality, against which our own becomes insignificant. In Behn's and Poulin's versions, we "vanish." In Garmey/Wilson and in Hammer/Jaeger we "dissolve." In MacIntyre, Boney, Oswald, and Flemming we "perish," though Cohn says flatly, "die." Elsewhere we are "consumed" or "crushed." No . . . Actually, we are compared. Young is right, then, to be in that mode, but he uses both "I couldn't survive" and "shrivel," a word I suspect is somewhat sexual. Gass is going to go with Leishman's "fade" yet try to suggest something other than muscle as the reason. However, Gass' "completer" is an interpretation. Already we can detect, in at least Behn, Garmey/Wilson, Boney, Miranda, and Cohn, a serious musical insensitivity. The utterly fatuous religious tone of "were I gathered to the glory" forces me to hope that, for this translator, the hunt is over.

Finally: *Denn das Schöne ist nichts als des Schrecklichen Anfang, den wir noch grade ertragen, und wir bewundern es so, weil es gelassen verschmäht, uns zu zerstören. Ein jeder Engel ist schrecklich.*

Leishman/Spender.   For Beauty's nothing but beginning of Terror we're still just able to bear, and why we adore it so is because it serenely disdains to destroy us. Each single angel is terrible.

Leishman.   For Beauty's nothing but beginning of Terror we're still just able to bear, and why we adore it so is because it serenely disdains to destroy us. Every angel is terrible.

Behn.
For beauty is only a seed of dread to be endured yet adored since it disdains to destroy us. An Angel alone, is misted in dread . . .

MacIntyre.
For beauty is nothing but the beginning of terror we can just barely endure, and we admire it so because it calmly disdains to destroy us. Every angel is terrible.

Garmey/Wilson.
For Beauty is only the beginning of a terror we can just barely endure, and what we so admire is its calm disdaining to destroy us. Every Angel brings terror.

Boney.
For Beauty is nothing but the beginning of awesomeness which we can barely endure and we marvel at it so because it calmly disdains to destroy us. Each and every angel is awesome.

Poulin.
Because beauty's nothing but the start of terror we can hardly bear, and we adore it because of the serene scorn it could kill us with. Every angel's terrifying.

Young.
Beauty is only the first touch of terror we can still bear and it awes us so much because it so coolly disdains to destroy us. Every single angel is terrible!

Miranda.
For Beauty is just the beginning of a terror we can barely stand: we admire it because it calmly refuses to crush us. Every angel terrifies.

Mitchell.
For beauty is nothing but the beginning of terror, which we still are just able to endure, and we are so awed because it

serenely disdains to annihilate us. Every angel is terrifying.

Flemming.

For beauty is nothing but the beginning of terror which we are barely able to endure and are awed because it serenely disdains to annihilate us. Each single angel is terrifying.

Hunter.

For Beauty is only the infant of scarcely endurable Terror, and we are amazed when it casually spares us. Every Angel is terrible.

Cohn.

Beauty is as close to terror as we can well endure. Angels would not condescend to damn our meagre souls. That is why they awe and why they terrify us so. Every angel is terrible!

Hammer/Jaeger.

But beauty's nothing but the start of that terror we can just manage to bear, and we're fascinated by it because it serenely scorns to destroy us. Every angel is terrifying.

Oswald.

For what strikes us as beauty is nothing but all we can bear of a terror's beginning, and we admire it so, because it calmly disdains to destroy us. Every angel strikes terror.

Gass.

For Beauty is nothing but the approach of a Terror we're only just able to bear, and we worship it so because it serenely disdains to destroy us. Every Angel is awesome.

We have barely begun our labors when we strike a passage which will warn us of the difficulties to come. The fifteen of us have already trampled over the poem's fresh snow, veering this way and that, and starting fearfully at the least thing. Now we have to stop "translating" and ask ourselves just what in the world the poet can mean. German obscurities and English obscurities do not rhyme.

Beauty is an objective attribute, terror is a subjective state. We must not identify them, or even claim they are "close," as Cohn does. Beauty cannot be the start or the beginning of a feeling, then, nor does it cause terror the way a coldcauses a cough. Nevertheless, when we see beauty we know that we shall feel terror shortly. It announces it. That's why I used the word "approach." Now, however, I think less of that selection, and, pushing the Annunciation imagery, I prefer to say that "Beauty is the herald of a Terror we're only just able to bear."

When the voice spoke the first line to him, Rilke had nearly completed his *Life of Mary* cycle, and his head was naturally full of the flutter of angel wings. Yet it is *his* barrenness that is overcome, not hers, and the angels who occupy the *Elegies* will not resemble any Mary may have known.

Edna St. Vincent Millay wrote that "Euclid alone has looked on beauty bare." Men are routinely blinded by the divine. Or they swoon. Or go mad. In this case, "it" disdains to destroy us. Rilke's vague pronouns, with their indefinite and ambiguous referents, are exasperating. Angels are the nearest we're ever going to get to pure Being. They resemble Leibniz's monads more than things-in-themselves. It is the intense reality of the Angels (signified by their Beauty) which terrifies us, casts us in the shade. What we adore is the indifference of the Angels, because they aren't about to clasp us to their "bosom." They will simply provide the opportunity for us to make the frightening comparison of their reality with ours.

Angels can't be terrible. Pot-holed roads are terrible. Times are terrible. The roast is terrible. Terrifying, yes . . . terrible . . .

no. "Awesome" is also a word being given the teenage treatment, but I think it is still possible to say "awesome," and not mean the noise from an electrolouded band.

Beauty, in Angels and elsewhere, is the revelation of a wholly inhuman perfection, for art, as Rilke wrote, goes against the grain of nature and transcends man. Just as, in Plato, any apprehension of the Forms is achieved through a deadly separation of the rational soul from the influence of the body, so in these *Elegies* a glimpse of such purity is possible only by means of a vertiginous breach in the self as might be made by a mighty quake of earth—one which can close as abruptly as it opened. Poulin's thought that it is scorn which might kill us strikes me as mistaken, since it is the sovereign remoteness of Beauty itself which prevents our destruction. "Kill" is metaphysically quite the wrong word, and its use suggests a basic failure on the translator's part to appreciate the momentous oracular tone of these mysterious and magnificent poems.

Leishman improves on his first try by replacing "Each single," which is redundant anyway, with "Every." We should certainly pay attention to what Leishman does because he has established his authority already; nevertheless, the elisions here ("For Beauty's [is] nothing but [the] beginning of [a] Terror") don't help the flow of the line at all, although for awkwardness, what could surpass the swan-like wobble of Flemming's "For beauty is nothing but the beginning of terror which we are barely able to endure and are awed because it serenely disdains to annihilate us"? MacIntyre also suffers from contractions, while Poulin continues to go for the colloquial, doubling "because," inserting the contraction, lowering the language, letting a line end slackly with "with." Prose has begun to creep over some versions like a vine. Gass, as usual, wants both the terror and the awesomeness of the Angels, but the "awesomeness" in Boney is awful. Behn, Hunter, and Cohn have already begun writing their own poem.

"Misted"? "Infant"? "Meagre"? May the Muses hurry them to their reward.

To this point the translators' task has been reasonably easy—which has not prevented a number of them from creating special difficulties of their own the way a drunk will bend the straightest road; and we may be at least allowed the suspicion that it is the translator's side of the equation which won't—which refuses to—total agreeably. Many translators do not bother to understand their texts. That would interfere with their own creativity and with their perception of what the poet ought to have said. They do not wish to become the trumpet through which another's breath blows, and indeed the English horn often overcomes its notes, so we hear *it*, not Wagner, so it's "its" sweetness which overcomes us, the way a rich syrup tops a sundae, and we easily miss the cool refinements of line and composition beneath the hot thick flow of tone.

And they would rather be original than right; they insist on repainting the stolen horse; "it's my translation," they say as they sign it, as if their work were the work of art. How should we fare if printers did the same, putting out their own *Lost Paradise*, their personalized versions of *As You Prefer It*? Love and honor to the shameless thief—one who doesn't care where his horse came from, or even if it looks like another's, so long as it runs in the money.

Translators are on a par with poets when it comes to being mean-spirited. Walter Arndt, in his arrogant collection called *The Best of Rilke* (there are no *Elegies*), complains bitterly about the efforts of others, and one can enjoy his diatribes, if not the poems themselves. Considering line 4 of the "Panther" poem, Arndt says of one esteemed translator,

the drugged languor of the stanza is spoiled, from mere ineptitude, by the indecent hop-and-skip of an anapaest.

Its rhymes, moreover, are replaced by assonances. Close assonances may be unavoidable second-bests occasionally, but to this pains-faking paraphrast they are neither close nor occasional but part of a cheery what-the-hellitude that Rilke, of all delicate spirits, has not deserved.[2]

Arndt is scornful of those who try to translate from a language to which they are not native, and there is no doubt that such a practice frequently leads to errors, some of which he properly points out, though we could use a little less gloat and glee, since he deals with every mistake as if he has caught a criminal. In my opinion, it is more important that the translator have native-like possession of the language into which he is trying to put his chosen poem. Arndt is also, I think, idolatrous about genre and meter and rhyme, and insists on twisting normal English orders inside out simply to satisfy a scheme.

I've already complained of how political it all is anyway. The poet, while composing, struggles to rule a nation of greedy self-serving malcontents; every idea, however tangential to the main theme it may have been initially, wants to submerge the central subject beneath its fructifying self as though each drizzle were scheming a forty-days rain; every jig and trot desires to be the whole dance; every la-di-da and line length, image, order, rhyme, variation, and refrain, every well-mouthed vowel, dental click, silent design, represents a corporation, cartel, union, well-heeled lobby, a Pentagon or NRA, eager to turn the law toward its interests; every word wants to enjoy a potency so supreme it will emasculate the others (I have known the little letter "a" to act just that outrageously); and then there is the poet too, who is supposed to be in charge, a fraud like Oz's Wizard, teetering on a paper throne and trying to keep a dozen personal insecurities from finding out about each other; trying to overcome the temptation to give in to one poetic demand at the expense of another—the Useful instead of the Alluring, the Alluring rather than what's Essential—trying to avoid habits which prefer first thoughts, indulge weak ones, encourage the facile, and ruin the work.

Thus the completed poem is a series of delicate adjudications, a peace created from contention, and there are occasionally those beautiful moments when every element runs together freely toward the same end and every citizen cries out, "Aye!" Must the translator mimic this mess, and take the measure of such miracles? He must. The translator, remaining in command of his best self while working in another unaccommodating language, must somehow register these decisions and adjustments, the many permissions and denials issued by the poet in the first place. The result, of course, is the record of a reading, and almost never a poem—not the economical setting down of a critical interpretation, although the interpretation must take place, but one step beyond that toward the compound, multi-spliced and engineered, performance which emerges from a recording studio. Still, to sing Rilke in English, even when machines have gloriously falsified your voice: *Ein Gott vermags.*

A god can do it. But tell me,
how can a man follow him through the lyre's strings?
His soul is split. And at the intersection
of two heart-riven roads, there is no temple to Apollo.

Song, as you have taught, is not mere longing,
the wooing of whatever lovely can be attained;
singing is being. Easy for a god.
But when are we? And when does he fill us

with earth and stars?
Young man, this isn't it, your yearning,
even if your voice bursts out of your mouth.

Learn to forget such impulsive song. It won't last.
Real singing takes another breath.
A breath made of nothing. Inhalation in a god. A wind.[3]

So find an English song for these words, these phrases, from
"Die Spanische Trilogie," for instance: . . . *der den Schein
zerrissner Himmels-Lichtung fängt* . . . , . . . *das grosse dunkle
Nichtmehrsein der Welt ausatmend hinnimmt* . . . , . . . *aus
schlaftrunknen Kindern an so fremder Brust* . . . , or, my favorite, . . . *wie ein Meteor in seiner Schwere nur die Summe Flugs
zusammennimmt.* . . . You don't have to know German. Just look
at it: *zusammennimmt.* A god can't do it.

Nor are poems approached in innocence, and with the
absence of lubricating forethought. Have we not had to suffer
those who direct *The Tempest* as if it took place in Central Park?
Many of our translators have programs—organized preconcep-
tions—which drive and direct their labors. Hölderlin must sound
as if written now. Why? The cry of the current is continuous like
a noisy creek; let's have a Hegel for our time, a Kant for the country club. Shall we throw Racine into a hearty street vernacular,
update Dido and Aeneas? Or if nostalgia overtakes us, we can run
as well in reverse. Does not MacIntyre translate *Weltraum* as
"welkin," down-dating Rilke in the direction of Chaucer?

Welcome to the pole vault. The second section of this "First
Elegy" puts the bar at twenty feet. *Und so verhalt ich mich denn
und verschlucke den Lockruf dunkelen Schluchzens.* Several
words from the opening line find re-employment. A harsh and
overwhelming music surrounds these bird-sung meanings, and
a deforming pattern, like a bound foot, unreasonably demands
to be danced.

Leishman/Spender. And so I keep down my heart, and swallow
the call-note of depth-dark sobbing.

Leishman.	And so I repress myself, and swallow the call-note of depth-dark sobbing.
MacIntyre.	And so I restrain myself and swallow the luring call of dark sobbing.
Garmey/Wilson.	So I withhold myself and keep back the lure of my dark sobbing.
Boney.	And so I restrain myself and suppress the luring call with somber sobs.
Poulin.	So I control myself and choke back the lure of my dark cry.
Young.	And since that's the case I choke back my own dark birdcall, my sobbing.
Mitchell.	So I hold myself back and swallow the call-note of my dark sobbing.
Flemming.	And so I force myself, swallow and hold back the surging call of my dark sobbing.
Gass 1.	And so I contain myself; choke back the appealing child's cry of my innermost part.
Gass 2.	And so I master myself and hold back the appealing outcry of my childhood heart.

If we try to stay close to the immediate English sense of the German words, a nearly vomitous calamity results (consider Leishman's unfortunate initial effort, for instance), and we must avoid these luring calls, these dark sobs, at all costs. The controlling image, which "The Third Elegy" confirms, is that of the frightened child calling for Mother to remove the darkness with its terror, which, like the absent light, is so alive in it. Thus the cry is an appealing one on two counts, and one which issues from the poet's deepest nature. The cry is held back because the fear itself is a fear we worship out of frightened gratitude; because the cry comes from the child in us; and because it is anyhow pointless, as the famous lines which follow mournfully but selfishly reiterate: alas, who is there we can make use of?

However, what does Rilke say the "call" is like? Although Young's casual prosiness is again inexplicable ("And since that's the case . . ."), he is the only translator to put Rilke's bird on its perch. The idea that the cry is effective the way a child's sobbing might be, and the notion that the cry is alluring as the mating calls of the bird are meant to be, collide like two trains. I see only smoke and steam. But Rilke likes to pass through all the ranks: not God, not Angels, not men, not birds either. Perhaps a tree or a walk or a habit, as we'll see, reading on, but our friends are few.

Gass 3. So I master myself to stifle an appealing outcry—instinctive as a mating song. Alas, who is there we can call on? Not Angels, not men, and even the observant animals are aware that we're not very happily home here, in this—our interpreted world.

"So I master myself to stifle" is awkward; " . . . instinctive as a mating song" is an interpretation, but at the moment I want to keep it because I think the bird has to be there. Birds coo sometimes, or moan, but they never sob.

Gass 4. So I master myself to muffle an appealing heart's cry—instinctive as a mating song. Alas, who is there we can call on?

Not another "heart," I can hear my inner critic saying, and too many m&m's. The pattern of alliteration could be shifted:

Gass 5. So I control myself to cut short an appealing outcry—
instinctive as a mating song. Alas, who is there we can
call on?

But "cut short" is a bit too colloquial, and too temporal to boot.
We're not talking about a vacation. "So I control myself to muffle an appealing outcry—"

As we advance into the elegy as into some movie Africa, the
weaknesses of our company become increasingly manifest: the
heat is getting to them, the rotten gin, the drums, the flies.
Who but fish swallow lures? Garmey/Wilson suggest that the
poet withholds himself, and Boney that the poet actually
employs his somber sobs to suppress his luring call. It is hard to
imagine a version much worse than my first try. Shall we permit
readers to believe that this great poem contains lines of such
pretentious silliness? Poulin's translation is cleaner than the
others, as is customary with him, and that is not a minor merit
when among the unwashed; yet for any poem, song is essential
to its being, and all we hear here are the squeaks of unoiled
doors. *Für den Gott ein Leichtes*. There is that wonderful
moment, for instance, when the poem asks lovers (who charac-
teristically believe their arms encircle an exciting and excited
body) to add the actual emptiness they are grasping to the totality of space (*Wirf aus den Armen die Leere zu den Räumen
hinzu, die wir atmen; vielleicht dass die Vögel die erweiterte Luft
fühlen mit innigerm Flug*), and Leishman gives us a triumphant
rendering:

Leishman. Fling the emptiness out of your arms to broaden the
spaces we breathe—maybe that [*sic*] the birds will
feel the extended air in more fervent flight.

Alongside this, Poulin's attempt is awkward and prosy, except that (like Garmey/Wilson) he emphasizes the interior meanings that apply to *innigerm*, always appropriate with Rilke.

Poulin.   Throw the emptiness in your arms out into that space we breathe; maybe birds will feel the air thinning as they fly deeper into themselves.

Poulin has no knack for the right word here. If we are hurling away from us what we've once hugged, isn't "fling" the only correct name for the gesture which empties our arms?
Mitchell is significantly better.

Mitchell.   Fling the emptiness out of your arms into the spaces we breathe; perhaps the birds will feel the expanded air with more passionate flying.

Gass, a jackal who comes along after the kill to nose over the uneaten hunks, keeps everything he likes:

Gass 1.   Fling the emptiness out of your arms to broaden the spaces we breathe—maybe then birds will feel the amplified air with an inner flight.
Gass 2.   Fling the emptiness out of your arms to broaden the spaces we breathe—maybe then birds will feel the amplified air with more fervent flight.

I am obliged to point out that Flemming, whose translation I came upon rather late in the day, also uses "fervent" to qualify "flight," but I wonder at his word order:

Flemming. Fling out of your arms the emptiness into the spaces we breathe—perhaps the birds will feel the expanded air in their more fervent flight.

As we pursue these comparisons tediously from line to line and verse to verse, it becomes evident that Leishman, Poulin, and Mitchell have given us the only tolerable versions, and that they are quite different in spirit as well as in the details of their execution. The awkwardness of Leishman's frequent Germanic constructions, his sometimes overly noisy line, the mumbo jumbo that gets into them, the oh-so-literary faces he makes, the occasional inaccuracy, the thickets of confusion we need to be rabbits to run through: we are certainly as familiar with these qualities now as with the faults of a friend, for J. B. Leishman, more than anyone else, has given us our poet, Rilke, in English (as Herter Norton has rendered the prose), and his lines have been impressed on our sensibilities like creases of bedclothing on sleeping bodies; it is impossible to remove them, especially when they dent so handsomely, and "immemorial sap mounts in our arms when we love." Yet he will do his derivative dances, like this Hopkins jig from "The Second Elegy":

Leishman.   Let the archangel perilous now, from behind the stars, step but a step down hitherwards: high up-beating, our heart would out-beat us. Who are you?

Poulin, our second, younger, far fresher horse, neatly reduces this to:

Poulin.   If the archangel, the dangerous one behind the stars, took just one step down toward us today: the quicker pounding of our heart would kill us. Who are you?

Meanwhile, Stephen Mitchell, presently our most popular translator of Rilke's work, goes back to Leishman, because Leishman is struggling to capture qualities in Rilke's lines that are really there, while Poulin quietly erases them. Mitchell achieves this improvement:

Mitchell.   But if the archangel now, perilous, from behind the stars took even one step down toward us: our own heart, beating higher and higher, would beat us to death. Who *are* you?

Before pushing my pencil angrily through the paper, I stumble through the passage first this way, then that:

Gass 1.   Were the perilous great Angel behind the stars to step down a single step toward us now, our stepped-up heart would overbeat and break us. Who are you?

Gass 2.   Yet if the archangel, perilous now, were to step but a step down toward us from behind the stars, our own heartbeaten heart would burst our chest. Who *are* you?

Poulin's and Mitchell's translations are frequently superior to Leishman's in terms of what they do not attempt. In "The Ninth Elegy," for instance, occurs the famous heart-and-hammer image:

Leishman.   Between the hammers lives on our heart, as between the teeth the tongue, which, in spite of all, still continues to praise.

Poulin.   Our heart survives between hammers, just as the tongue between the teeth is still able to praise.

Mitchell.   Between the hammers our heart endures, just as the tongue does between the teeth and, despite that, still is able to praise.

78

Gass.   Our heart dwells between hammers, like the tongue
          between the teeth, where it remains, notwithstand-
          ing, a continual creator of praise.

Leishman lets the German twist his line. Poulin's row has a better bite, like straightened teeth, but he finishes too quickly.

Images like this—of a space enlarged by the emptiness in a
lover's arms; of a bat ricocheting through the air like a crack
through a cup; of a child's death made from gray bread and
stuffed in the child's mouth like the core of an apple . . . no . . .
like the ragged core of a sweet apple; or the ideas themselves:
that the world exists nowhere but within and therefore the
springtimes have need of us; that the youthfully dead have a
special meaning and life and death run like hot and cold
through the same tap; that we are here just to speak and proclaim the word; that love should give its beloved an unfastening
and enabling freedom; that praise is the thing—they belong to
no language, but to the realm of absolute image and pure idea,
where a simple thought or bare proportion can retain its ele-
mentary power; and it is the ubiquitous presence of these type-
tropes and generalizing "ideas" in Rilke that makes translating
him possible at all, as their relative absence in someone like
Mallarmé makes him as difficult to shape as smoke.

Poulin is uncomfortable, not with the rough free form of the
Elegies, but with their metaphysical grandeur. The lighter
translucency of the *Sonnets to Orpheus* is more to his liking,
while Leishman's tread there is too heavy, still too elegiac, even
in his most successful moments, as if he had continued to slog
long after the swamp had dried and its residual dusts had blown.

The trials of the translator can contain no better testimony
that they are trials indeed than the abrupt and thrilling opening
of the *Sonnets to Orpheus*, an opening which so beautifully
describes the poems themselves: *Da stieg ein Baum.*

Leishman.	A tree ascending there. O pure transcension! O Orpheus sings! O tall tree in the ear!
MacIntyre.	There arose a tree. Oh, pure transcension! Oh, Orpheus sings! Oh, tall tree in the ear!
Pitchford.	Somewhere a tree ascended. Oh sheer transcendence. Oh Orpheus singing. Oh tall tree lofted in the ear.
Poulin.	A tree sprang up. O sheer transcendence! O Orpheus sings! O tall tree in the ear!
Mitchell.	A tree ascended there. Oh pure transcendence! Oh Orpheus sings! Oh tall tree in the ear!
Flemming.	There rose a tree. O magic transcendence! Orpheus sings. And in the ear a tree!
Norton.	There rose a tree. O pure transcendency! O Orpheus singing! O tall tree in the ear!
Gass 1.	A suddenly ascending tree. O pure transcendency! O Orpheus sings! O tall tree in the ear!

Merit is spread pretty evenly here. Except for Pitchford's "Somewhere a tree ascended." Actually, this tree shoots up in a special way—it does not simply rise. Instead of being climbed, it does the climbing—it scales the sky—and in that lies its transcendence. Both Leishman and Gass are after a kind of "going up." Gass, who flails like someone drowning here, found the word which would reflect that rising music, but the word was "scaled," and no one wants to keep company with flaking and disease. "There climbed a tree" or "There scaled a tree" are silly in English. Yet "scaled" is so nearly the right word. A bitter business, this. Poulin puts the suddenness in the verb, a good idea, while Gass expansively explains it. MacIntyre's rocky rhythm prevents any real rising (arose / a tree). Gass, again, defeats his own sense with an overlong line. Both MacIntyre and Mitchell seem insensitive to the differences between "O" and "Oh" and

"Oh,". To find a tree in your ear is odd enough, but Flemming almost sticks it in there. Pitchford postpones the problem. In English, one exclaims: "Oh rats!" or "Oh my God!" but never "Oh transubstantiation!" Though "transcendency" goes better with "tree" than its other forms do. Between Leishman, Poulin, and Norton, it is difficult to choose, although Poulin is more natural in English. There is nevertheless something satisfactory about Norton's honest literalism.

So Orpheus sings, and a tall tree springs up in the ear. This pure wand of song creates a clearing into which charmed animals are drawn to listen to Orpheus, who could move the trees as well as the wind. We must forbid the image to remind us of Disney.

Leishman. Creatures of silence pressing through the clear disintricated wood from lair and nest . . .

MacIntyre. Animals from the silence, from the clear now opened wood came forth from nest and den . . .

Pitchford. Out of such quiet, out of each lair and nest, animals crept from their disenchanted wood . . .

Poulin. Creatures of silence crowded out of the clear freed forest, out of their dens and lairs . . .

Mitchell. Creatures of stillness crowded from the bright unbound forest, out of their lairs and nests . . .

Flemming. For creatures stepped soundlessly from clearings of forests and left lair and nest behind . . .

Norton. Creatures of stillness thronged out of the clear released wood from lair and nesting place . . .

"Disintricated" is an inspired Shakespearean coinage, but the word it replaces is *gelösten* (with its twin suggestion of "listen" and "loosen"), and we are no longer in those intricated elegies where the compaction would have been appropriate. Leishman and MacIntyre preserve the rhyme scheme of the original (as they attempt to do throughout), yet it is a strange sort of preservation which so often forces the English into grotesque shapes. Poulin and Norton have a better plan. They allow rhyme to occur as the sense of the language readily permits it, suggesting the sonnet form rather than duplicating it. Flemming's emphasis (stressing what the animals left behind) is all wrong, and his lines are as painful as walking in a tight boot. Pitchford claims the woods have been disenchanted when exactly the opposite has happened. The forests are confining until Orpheus' enchanting music releases them. Poulin's "freed forest" is fine. His version is clearly superior in every respect.

Skipping a few lines:

Leishman.   And where before
less than a hut had harboured what came thronging,
a refuge tunneled out of dimmest longing
with lowly entrance through a quivering door,
you built them temples in their sense of sound.

MacIntyre.   Where scarce a humble
hut for such reception was before,
a hiding-place of the obscurest yearning,
with entrance shaft whose underpinnings tremble,
you made for the beasts temples in their hearing.

Pitchford.   And where hardly a hut
had stood to receive and shelter this, you made
a secret burrow out of the darkest need,
an opening on which strung columns vibrate,
you built a temple for them out of hearing.

Poulin.   And where there'd been
hardly a hut before to take this in,
a dugout carved from their darkest desire

                    with a lintel of trembling timber—
                    you erected temples for them in their inner ear.
Mitchell.   And where there had been
                    just a makeshift hut to receive the music,
                    a shelter nailed up out of their darkest longing,
                    with an entryway that shuddered in the wind—
                    you built a temple deep inside their hearing.
Flemming.   And where
                    there was scarcely a hut to shelter them,—
                    a hiding place out of their darkest longings,
                    there you created temples in their ears.
Norton.   And where before
                    hardly a hut had been to take this in,
                    a covert out of darkest longing
                    with an entrance way whose timbers tremble,—
                    you built temples for them in their hearing.

For everyone but Poulin the poem falls into artificial pieces, as
if the loosened petals of a real rose turned to plastic as they
reached the ground. Leishman's "quivering door" is a disaster;
moreover, the language is as puffy as a dissipated face. Norton
is always a help for those who need a pony, but this time the
animal is too young to ride. I would rather Poulin had used a
den instead of a dugout, since a canoe doesn't belong here. My
final try follows:

                    There rose a tree. O pure uprising!
                    O Orpheus sings! O tall tree in the ear!
                    And hushed all things. Yet even in that silence
                    a new beginning, beckoning, new bent appeared.

                    Creatures of silence thronged from the clear
                    released trees, out of their lairs and nests,

and their quiet was not the consequence
of any cunning, any fear,

but was because of listening. Growl, shriek, roar,
shrank to the size of their hearts. And where there'd been
ramshackles to shelter such sounds before—

just dens designed from their darkest desires,
with doorways whose doorposts trembled—
you built a temple in the precincts of their hearing.[4]

The *Sonnets* are written in a light, flowing, yet terribly condensed language of incredible musicality, verbal playfulness, and sudden invention. Metamorphosis is their mode of operation. What is one to do with Rilke's management of "*i*" and "*e*" in that overpowering first line: *Da stieg ein Baum. O reine übersteigung!* or with the way the third line picks it up: *Und alles schwieg. Doch seibst in der Verschweigung . . . ?* One can do nothing, only try to enrich one's own poor transcription wherever possible and by whatever harmonious means will work.

It may seem perverse, but the translator must, I think, avoid construing: a tree is a kind of vegetable bridge between earth and sky, the immanent and the transcendent. It is a tree like those of the forest, yet it is made of music. It is this . . . It is that . . . Soon I may know too much for my own good, and be tempted to offer the reader an apple from my tree of knowledge. One is generally wise to render the poem as the poet wrote it and let the poet's poem explain itself. Generally . . .

2

It was nearly a girl who went forth
from this joyful union of song and lyre,

and shone so clearly through the veils of her youth,
and made herself a bed within my ear.

And slept in me. And all slept inside her sleep:
the trees which had always amazed me,
meadow-deep distances as touchable as skin,
and every astonishment that has ever been.

She slept the world. Singing God,
how could you have made her so complete
she never wanted to be first awake?
See: she rose and slept.

Where is her death? O will you find the hidden theme
before your song sings its own grave?
From me—where does she fade to? still nearly a girl . . . ⁵

The first set of *Sonnets* appeared unbidden before the
remainder of the *Elegies* was given. The second set is written
with the exhilarating knowledge that the *Elegies* exist. There's II,
17, for instance:

Leishman. Where, in what ever-blissfully watered gardens,
upon what trees, out of, oh, what gently dispetalled
flower-cups do these so strange-looking fruits of
consolation mature?

MacIntyre. Where, in what ever-happily watered garden, on
what trees, from what tenderly stripped flower-
calices ripen the strange fruits of consolation?

Pitchford. Where, in what forever mercifully drenched gardens, in what trees, out of what defoliated bud-
calyxes, once so delicate, do the rare fruits of
compassion ripen?

Poulin.   Where, in what heavenly watered gardens, in
             what trees, from what lovingly unsheathed
             flower-calyxes do the strange fruits of consolation
             ripen?
Norton.   Where, in what ever-blessedly watered gardens,
             on what trees, out of what tenderly unleaved
             blossom-calyxes do the exotic fruits of consolation
             ripen?
Spiers.   Where, in whichever blissfully watered gardens, on
             which Trees, and out of which tenderly unpetaled
             flower cups Do they ripen, the strange fruits of
             consolation?

Leishman is sappy. MacIntyre is insipid. Pitchford has never
heard of Vietnam. Poulin's "heavenly" is an instant improvement over "bless" and "bliss." I don't think Rilke means the
fruits of consolation to be exotic—strange, yes, even alien—
though it is their trees that are faraway and foreign. These
poems, these fruits, are strange because they are unbidden. And
Eden was long ago closed for repairs. Spiers replaces the word
"what" with the word "which"—why? However, her "unpetaled
flower cups" seems the most natural and least forced. In German, the prepositional march from *in* to *an* through *aus* is terribly important, and yet Poulin (alone) ignores it. One is tempted
to resort to the kind of explanation I just warned about: Where,
in what beautifully cared-for gardens, on what inspired trees,
from what gently unpetaled flower cups do these unexpected
fruits of consolation ripen?

If we had been choosing chocolates, this last one would have
been a jelly. "Forever mercifully drenched" indeed. Let's put its
partly bitten body back and try another piece just a little earlier
in the row: 11, 13.

Leishman. Anticipate all farewells, as were they behind you now, like the winter going past. For through some winter you feel such wintriness bind you, your then out-wintering heart will always outlast.

MacIntyre. Keep ahead of all parting, as if it were behind you, like the winter that is just now passed. In winters you are so endlessly winter, you find that, getting through winter, your heart on the whole will last.

Poulin. Be ahead of all Departure, as if it were behind you like the winter that's just passed. For among winters there's one so endlessly winter that, wintering out, your heart will really last.

Mitchell. Be ahead of all parting, as though it already were behind you, like the winter that has just gone by. For among these winters there is one so endlessly winter that only by wintering through it will your heart survive.

Norton. Be in advance of all parting, as though it were behind you like the winter that is just going. For among winters one is so endlessly winter that, overwintering, your heart once for all will hold out.

This is one of the great sonnets, one of the most typically Rilkean in theme, too, one of the most moving—Epictetus might have penned it—and a poem quite impossible to translate. There is first of all the contrast between "ahead" and "behind," which MacIntyre and Poulin retain, but at their peril because the idea is really best expressed simply as Leishman does: "Anticipate all farewells." Four "winters" follow, and in the last line, three *übers*. All five of our contestants put in every one of these winters, some more smoothly than others (Poulin is clearly first), but Leishman, always fearless, forces two "outs" into the final line of the quatrain, though the strain is such that the poem sweats. No Sweat is clearly Poulin's motto, and for the *Sonnets* it is clearly a good one. His thought is clean and direct, and the positive poetry of that thought is simply allowed to have its effect. MacIntyre bungles things badly, arriving at a rhyme with a line so long it circles the moon, reducing his rhythms to those of poor prose, and badly bollixing the meaning. It is high time we closed the book on him.

"Be dead forever in Eurydice—" the following quatrain begins. What can that mean? Possibly: since you looked back and cost her her chance at resurrection, then you ought to "Remain with Eurydice in the realm of death." Mitchell interprets the lines plausibly: "Be forever dead in Eurydice— more gladly arise into the seamless life proclaimed in your song," although that's not exactly Rilke's wording. What to do?

Anticipate all farewells, as if they were behind you
like the winter that's just past, for among winters
there will be one so relentlessly winter
that in overwintering it your heart will be readied to last.

Remain with Eurydice in the realm of death—rise there
singing, praising, to realize the harmony in your strings.
Here—among pale shades in a fading world—
be a ringing glass that shatters as it rings.

Be—but nonetheless know why nothingness
is the unending source of your most fervent vibration,
so that this once you may give it your full affirmation.

> To the store of copious Nature's used-up, cast-off,
> speechless creatures—an unsayable amount—
> jubilantly join yourself and cancel the count.[6]

I hate "vibration/affirmation" but, so far, I haven't been able to improve on it. This triplet is tough to render in reasonably uninflated English.

For every poet we attempt to translate, certain adjustments will have to be made, equivalences found, sacrifices accepted; and we shall have to decide in each instance (whether the poet is Valéry or Hölderlin, Vallejo or Montale—whether the issue is rhythm, verse form, figures, sound, or wordplay—ambiguity, syntax, idea, or tone—diction, subject, weight, ambition— secret grief, overmastering obsession) just what element is so essential that a literal transcription must be aimed at; what we dare to seek certain equivalences for instead; when we can afford to settle for similar general impressions and effect; how to unpack the overly compacted; and what must be let go, unless luck is with us, in order to achieve the rest—that rest which must add up to greatness; and in the case of Rilke, I think, the poetry of idea must come first, the metaphors he makes out of the very edge and absence of meaning, the intense metaphysical quality of his vision (as unphilosophically developed as it yet is); while tone and overall effect would be next— in the *Elegies* that prophetic grandeur some of his translators are not convinced of—Rilke's hubristic ambition, the vanity of "the seer"—and in the *Sonnets* the quick hot Heraclitean quality of a flame in which others have been unwilling to hold their hands without wincing (II, 12):

> Will transformation. Be inspired by the flame
> where a thing made of change conceals itself.

then the figures, so essential, and some sense of Rilke's rich verbal music, complex wordplay, and intricate complicities of suggestion; so that reaching the last factor, I think I'd be ready, in most cases, to give up his verse forms first.

Most of the translators of the *Elegies* and the *Sonnets* do their homework and offer useful notes. There are certainly many clues to the meaning of Rilke's poems to be found in his letters. Above all, nearly every poem is a version of many poems that have been written before it, and of many more to follow. This is one reason why Rilke is given to poetic outbursts. These sudden outpourings are summations: the regathering, reclenching, and releasing of a fresh fistful of former themes, images, motifs, emotions, ideas.

Yet in several significant instances, scholarship has failed to warn translators away from errors. The most outrageous of these occurs in the first quatrain of a very famous sonnet from *New Poems*, "Torso of an Archaic Apollo." In a footnote in his *Rainer Maria Rilke: Selected Works*,[7] Leishman explains that in Germany and Austria the word *Kandelaber* "was the usual word for a streetlamp: not for the comparatively short post with a single square lantern, but for the much taller and more elegant sort with two globes, each suspended from either end of a wide semicircular crosspiece. Gas lamps, in which the main supply was turned on by means of a long pole and ignited from a small, perpetually burning bypass, had not yet been replaced by electric. Rilke had already used the word in the poem 'Night Drive.' "

This news comes too late to help C. F. MacIntyre, who is forced into contortions:

> Never will we know his fabulous head
> where the eyes' apples slowly ripened. Yet

his torso glows: a candelabrum set
before his gaze which is pushed back and hid . . .

Even Leishman concentrates on the second part of his information (how the gas is turned down), instead of on the shape of the
lamps, with their semicircular, hence skull-like, crosspiece and
their eye-shaped globes. He writes, omitting mention of the
Augenäpfel:

> Though we've not known his unimagined head
> and what divinity his eyes were showing,
> his torso like a branching street-lamp's glowing,
> wherein his gaze, only turned down, can shed
> light still.

My own effort tries, perhaps too hard, to justify itself:

> Never will we know his legendary head
> where the eyes' apples slowly ripened. Yet
> his torso glows as if his look were set
> above it in suspended globes that shed
> a street's light down.

The temptation to push past Rilke's German into the Platonic
poem itself, the poem no one can write without resorting to
some inevitably distorting language, is sometimes irresistible.
One should never go, I think, quite all the way, yet a little
flirting, some heavy petting, may sometimes be more than a
pleasant indulgence. Robert Lowell, Ezra Pound, or the gods
may succeed. To do so, the translator has to say to the reader:

forget the fact that the poem belongs in its body as utterly as you do in yours; listen to what's going on behind my tongue, in my mind where the Muse was, in your mind where the Muse is. Try to realize the presence of Apollo's decapitated head, its absent eyelight shining down upon the fragment that is its torso. See how complete this desecrated stone is, although it has no face, no smile, once upon a time tight curls of hair maybe, now armless, no longer wearing its inoffensive little phallus like a bit of fatter pubic hair, its well-muscled legs once extending into a firmly footed stance. They are the same bodily implements you have, reader (excepting, sometimes, the sex), without the necessity to imagine them, and none of them stone. Yet, lo and behold, that absent look, that vanished smile, is bright, and burns your eyes as you perceive its shine, flashing from this broken body to confront your inner incompleteness and condemn it. Are you as real as this ancient, battered remnant of statue? Change, then. Change your life.

> Never will we know his legendary head
> where the eyes' apples slowly ripened. Yet
> his torso glows as if his look were set
> above it in suspended globes that shed
>
> a street's light down. Otherwise the surging breast
> would not thus blind you, nor through the soft turn
> of the loins could you feel his smile pass easily
> into the bright groins where the genitals yearned.
>
> Otherwise this stone would not be so complete,
> from its shoulder showering body into absent feet,
> or seem as sleek and ripe as the pelt of a beast;

nor would that gaze be gathered up by every surface
to burst out blazing like a star, for there's no place
that does not see you. You must change your life.[8]

As the *Elegies* argue: the beauty of perfection, when we are
granted the doubtful good fortune to grasp it, announces the
reappearance of our fearful conviction that we are, in both the
soul and body of our being, so much less.

INHALATION IN A GOD

The *Duino Elegies* were not written; they were awaited. They were intended to be oracular and inspired. Their Being was to be beyond the poem. They are addressed first to the poet and then, as if over his shoulder, to the rest of us. Their language, like the radiance of the Angels so frequently invoked, streams forth from an ego, an "I," only to return again as a "you." They are, in that sense, enclosed, and if the reader resists the enclosure, he will never realize their nature. The *Elegies* are like the Angels in another way, then: they have only an inside. Which is the same as saying, "Their form is imaginary."

They came to him as if they already existed—all ten—the way a mural might exist; but he sees, at first, only bits and pieces, obtains a brief glimpse, only to have them covered again. They come numbered. They arrive in shards with little tags as if they had been taken out of a dig and carefully brushed off by dutiful students.

Their arrival was inevitable. The surprise was when.

To my mind, the most persuasive explanation of the phenomenon we are pleased to call "inspiration" (pleased because we like mysteries, we like to think ourselves chosen) is the one offered us by the mathematician Henri Poincaré in a little essay, "Mathematical Creation," frequently reprinted from his illuminating book *Foundations of Science*.

The ground must be there. The ground is an individual's genetic facility with the medium. But we must not be mistaken about what this facility is. Poincaré is at pains to point out that an inborn knack with numbers (a ready memory for such operations) has little to do with mathematical creativity. Nor does the ability many have to pick up languages as if the languages were thumbing a ride (again, a ready memory, a gift Rilke also had) give promise of poetry or playwriting or any other creative work. The ground Poincaré is speaking of is the ability to make fruitful connections between otherwise unlinked elements of the medium—mathematical connections in his case—resemblances, parallels, analogies—which constitute the synthesizing side of the science or the art; as well as the analytic aspect—the ability to discern deep differences among things as apparently similar as twins.

If the ground is there, we can begin to till it. The elements of the medium must be internalized. The principles of their manipulation must be mastered. Again, we must not confuse learning a language with the training necessary for its poetic use, precisely because the poetic use is a radical reversal of its function in ordinary life. Paradoxically, our budding poet must be "trained" to "play." If both rules and elements are few in number (as, relatively, they are in music, mathematics, and the formalized genres of poetry, and as they are definitely not in fiction, history, anthropology, or philosophy), then useful results may be possible, even expected, by youthful efforts in these fields.

The training does not conclude with the internalization of elements and rules. The practice of other mathematicians, or poets, or composers, must be studied, heard, consumed. This listening, this reading, must be of the analytical kind I have called (in the case of language) transreading. For what is crucial to creativity is the repeated experience, by our young practitioner, of quality of the highest kind. Really gifted people know that values are as "out there" as cows in a field. And a sense for such significant combinations must be developed. Creativity concerns correct choice. I should say that the whole nature of a culture can be seen in its patterns of selection. The entire history of both art and science supports the view that some choices are better than others.

What does one learn? To ask the right question. As I noted in the section on transreading, Leibniz's principle of sufficient reason in effect asks it: namely, why is a thing what it is, and not some other thing; or, why was this word chosen rather than some other? It may be that the nature of the universe does not provide answers of such completeness, so that we are left with half an explanation (what a thing is, not why it could not be otherwise), but works of art are supposed to bear more justification for their existence than you or I, a fox or flower or blade of grass, have to. There could be causes for the cosmos, but no reasons, or all of IT and the whole of WE could be accidents. The artist must do a better job than God has, although, having internalized the reasons for his choices, he may not be easily able to articulate them. Nevertheless, they'll be there.

What proper reading confers upon the right reader is not merely an expanded vocabulary or its subtle understanding, or the ready use of forms and strategies, but also a sympathetic awareness of traditional attitudes and opinions, feelings and desires. The young composer, the young poet, can, in this way, appear far wiser than his or her years. Alexander Pope says that he wrote the following poem at the age of twelve, and it scarcely matters to my point if he's cheating by a few years.

ODE ON SOLITUDE

Happy the man, whose wish and care
A few paternal acres bound,
Content to breathe his native air,
                In his own ground.

Whose herds with milk, whose fields with bread,
Whose flocks supply him with attire,
Whose trees in summer yield him shade,
                In winter fire.

Blest! who can unconcern'dly find
Hours, days, and years slide soft away,
In health of body, peace of mind,
                Quiet by day,

Sound sleep by night; study and ease
Together mix'd; sweet recreation,
And innocence, which most does please,
                With meditation.

Thus let me live, unseen, unknown;
Thus unlamented let me dye;
Steal from the world, and not a stone
                Tell where I lye.[1]

Does the kid really want to steal unsung, unpraised, and unheroic from the world? His attitudes are as borrowed as his forms and phrases. "Happy the man" indeed. But poems don't have to be sincere. They only need to be good.

After training (and Pope imitates the Earl of Rochester, Waller, Cowley, Spenser, Dorset; he translates Ovid and paraphrases Thomas à Kempis), after an education, comes practice. Intense. Extended. Mindful. Careful. While continuing to read, to imitate if necessary, to learn. Rilke's easy way with words led him astray, and he was late in his mastery of Goethe, Hölderlin, and many others. Rilke's salad days were followed by arid stretches, by doubts, difficulties of all kinds, and these were painful for him, but no doubt necessary. Meanwhile, he was trying to understand his own conflicted nature. It is important to remember that the body fuels the mind. And that character controls both. The creative life of the mathematician is usually over by age forty. Perhaps the emotional problems the scholar is fleeing, by working in a world of total abstraction, no longer exert the same fearful pressures. Rilke needed his neuroses, he thought, and he refused, for that reason, to undergo psychoanalysis, although it was suggested to him.

Once one has become a mathematician, a physicist, a poet, then what one knows, what one feels and thinks, can be focused upon a particular problem. "For fifteen days," Poincaré tells us, "I strove to prove that there could not be any functions like those I have since called Fuchsian functions." Despite his own denials, a sleepless night full of colliding ideas allowed him to establish the existence of such a class. Next, he wished to represent these new functions through the quotient of two series. This was a conscious choice. And the choice was made by an analogy with solutions achieved in other areas. Meanwhile, Poincaré had agreed to go by bus on a geologic excursion. Mathematical issues were far from his thoughts. "At the moment when I put my foot on the step [of the bus] the idea came to me, without anything in my former thoughts seeming to have paved the way for it, that the transformations I had used to define the Fuchsian functions were identical with those of non-Euclidean geometry."

As in Rilke's case, the ultimate solution to this complex problem was achieved in stages. Work. Blockage. Insight. Verification. Followed by the orderly development of the new idea.

Poincaré then turned his attention to what appeared to be quite a different set of problems in arithmetic, but he had a signal lack of success. Giving up in disgust, he took a few days off to visit the seaside. Then, for him, the Rilke-like moment arrived: "One morning, walking on the bluff, the idea came to me, with just the same characteristics of brevity, suddenness and immediate certainty, that the arithmetic transformations of indeterminate ternary quadratic forms were identical with those of non-Euclidean geometry." Further verifications follow. That is to say: proofs. "Naturally I set myself to form all these functions. I made a systematic attack upon them and carried all the outworks, one after another. There was one however that still held out, whose fall would involve that of the whole place." One more blockage. Now he has to leave his work to go through military service (Poincaré is no exception to the rule of youth). While he was walking down the street one seemingly ordinary day, "the solution of the difficulty which had stopped me suddenly appeared to me." He had to delay writing down this solution for some time, but time was no longer a factor. Eventually, he did it with dispatch.

In each stage of Poincaré's amazing discovery, there are the same factors: initial talent, life preparation, focus, failure, distraction, revelation. In Rilke's case, we can be considerably more detailed in our description. And the delays are sometimes years rather than weeks or days. Not only is the inspirational moment preceded by a lifetime of practice, but its environmental conditions must be fully met—in effect, the gun must be loaded and cocked before the trigger is pulled. However, since one is never sure what all these conditions are, they are realized by luck as much as plan.

Rilke has been reading Hölderlin again, and studying with admiration Goethe's *Roman Elegies*, soaking his soul in the distich, the poetry of the flute, rather than that of the lyre. His own practice will be irregular and free, but the rhythm is nevertheless fundamentally there: a foot which always falls, the dactyl ($|\smile$), and a pair of lines which does the same, dropping from six feet to five. Rilke's *Elegies* will end when happiness falls. The human faculty the *Elegies* invoke is memory, since their subject is loss, but this gives them distance, makes them meditative. The problems the *Elegies* address are not removable. Their mood is one of quiet mourning, of sober lamentation, then, because they are concerned to sing a sorrow no longer immediate and sharp, but one full of conciliation, acceptance, and repose.

Rilke's *Elegies* do not weep for Adonais, and nature is too indifferent to mankind's plight to make mountains frown or the sky shed tears. The "I" of the *Duino Elegies* is the "I" we all are: not mankind en masse, but "we" one after the other. Although some of the poetic personae of the *Elegies* are present in "Lament," written in Paris just before the fatal August of 1914— "heart," "lament," "tree," "angels," and not excluding the important condition of invisibility—the poem is about no one else than its author. It is a grim summing up, and hardly elegiac.

Who will you complain to, my heart? Your forsaken path
struggles on through the insensible mass of mankind.
All the more futile, perhaps, for maintaining its aim,
pushing on toward a future already lost.

Once before. You lamented? What was it for? A fallen
   unripe

berry of celebration. But now the entire tree is being
   broken,
by the storm it is shaken, my slowly grown tree of
   celebration.
Loveliest in my invisible
landscape, you that made me better known
to the also invisible angels.[2]

For the fully fledged elegy we need a mountain at whose peak we shall look down upon the world and try to find our place in it, though we stand atiptop while we do. And a tutelary spirit of feminine gender will also be required to attend us while we philosophize. The German name for this sort of thing is *Bildung*, and perhaps the most famous example is Schiller's "Der Spaziergang," an elegy sometimes felt to initiate the genre. In the tenth of the *Duino Elegies* we shall get our tutelary spirit and our mountain, too, however the metaphysical bent of the *Elegies* involves a far more general point of view than *Bildung* does.

Nevertheless (and this is I think a real oddity), the *Elegies*, because they resemble a revelation, are so utterly identified with the moment of their initial onset that the Duino cliffs and the bora which is cleansing the battlements are a part of the poem, are where the voice is heard, are where we are when we read and hear them. Mouth them, actually, for these poems are the most oral I know; they are meant not only to be listened to as one listens to, say, Wallace Stevens, but they must be spoken—not merely by but for yourself, as if you were the one who wondered whether you had anyone you could call to, anything you could, in your condition, make use of. This demand—that the reader become the poem—is there, even in translation, in any decent version, for the voice-making quality of these lines goes beyond their music. They are an utterance.

To sharpen my point: James Joyce's various Anna Livia Plurabelles are certainly as musical as prose gets, literally lilting on all the time, and they, too, ask to be performed, as most great prose and all great poetry does. But we perform them in order to *hear* them. We perform the *Elegies* in order to *say* them. To make their words ours.

Nor does the wanderer bring down a handful of earth
from his high mountain slope to the valley (for earth, too, is
    mute),
but a word he has plucked from the climbing: the yellow and
    blue
gentian. Are we, perhaps, *here* just to utter: house,
bridge, fountain, gate, jug, fruit tree, window—
at most: column, tower . . . but to *utter* them, remember,
to speak in a way which the named never dreamed
they could be.[3]

And to speak in a way we never dreamed we could speak.

We must add, then, to such mental preparation for the final inundation as the reading of Goethe and Hölderlin, Rilke's installation in the tower of Muzot. Not a castle, though the Germans will call a shoebox a *Schloss*, but a quadrangular tower at least, on a mountain slope, lifting its crenellated roof up into the trees, and boasting a view across a ravine and down toward a tiny town. It contained a lot of dinky rooms, three to each of its three stories, their windows set higgledy-piggledy across Muzot's face; yet it also possessed a tower . . . a tower of which Yeats would have been proud. Covered for many months by Swiss snow, at a place not easily reached, in a climate which forced solitude even on its atmosphere, engulfed by a landscape rich and various, in winter surrounded by white-fingered fruit trees, Muzot provided a security unusual for Rilke, and at long last.

The season is also suitable. January and February are the poet's best months. The first two *Elegies* entered him at Duino in January, but they were also preceded by the poems which constituted *The Life of Mary*, extending that exclamatory time. To be followed then by anxiety and sadness. Because Desperation is another preparation for inspiration, and Rilke was to have years of desperation: initially in Paris, where he suffered it while in the tolls of his *Notebooks*, and again in the tens of towns and in the scores of borrowed rooms where he dwelled during the decade sombered by the war, a decade which began shortly after the *Elegies* announced themselves.

The Duino outburst had made Rilke at first fancy he was like St. John receiving the *Apocalypse* on Patmos (remembering Hölderlin's majestic poem as he would a decade later), only to be cast back into a disappointing silence as he was by the grim castle most times in any case. "Near," Hölderlin begins, "Near and hard to grasp is God." The revelation had been too partial, perhaps premature, and even when Rilke ran naked along the seashore, his face in the wind as it had been on the parapet, the *Elegies* did not reannounce themselves. Rilke hid in the castle's large but undisciplined library and considered exploring its rich collection of Venetian material in order, perhaps, to write a biography of Admiral Carlo Zeno, whose great age (eighty-four at his death in 1418) invited a long look back (by a poet who was thirty-eight) ... yet at what? ... if not at growing old and becoming faintly quaint. His letters multiplied and lengthened, as did his desperations. When you have no daily work to go to, to stabilize your life and make it useful, especially when you are like a ghost caught in daylight; when there is no protective routine with its reassuring tedium to lull the nerves, and no one about to get on them either; then you go to hell instead; and Rilke found himself in rooms full of his previous pacing, everywhere in front of him volumes he'd pulled from their shelves but part way; and in some corner that he had neglected, unresolved problems were seated like judges in robes; what to do about his divorce from Clara; how to escape his enigmatic lovelife—in Rome entangled with Sidonie Nádherný von Borutin ("Sidie," a shortening dearly needed), while in Venice beset by Mimi Romanelli—and consequently how to cleanse his consciousness of guilt and distraction; next how to avoid sliding further into the generous hands of the Princess Marie or her closing social circle; moreover, what to do or where to go in order to escape those migraines that troubled one end of him and the hemorrhoids that pained the other; because, if the sirocco and the bora were insufferable at Duino, there was the foehn to make Munich miserable, not to omit most of Switzerland, and his neuroses to ruin the rest.

Rilke's teeth ached. He had little strength. He woke with stiff joints. According to Freedman, he felt as if lemon juice had been squeezed into his blood. Still, at the suggestion of the princess, he tried to put her library in order, and stood staring at its stacks instead. The princess, discerning his difficulties—and after a period when he ricocheted between Duino and Venice, driven there by ill-formed plans, drawn back by hesitations—generously offered him her *mezzanino* in the Palazzo Valmarana, where Rilke might enjoy its luxurious appointments, its wide views of the Grand Canal, while practicing much-needed economies. Rilke wanted to be Spartan, and refused. Finally, out of sorts and out of sous, he accepted. His head was soon clogged with society like a sinus.

Rilke was as restless as one who hoped to leave his pain in the parlor when he enters the dining room, and his worries in the bedroom when he comes down for breakfast, only to find them spread over his toast and clouding every view. This condition was common, and appeared to announce another flight, yet before Rilke could flee with his Muse to Spain, he fell into a friendship with Eleonora Duse, whose theatricalized life absorbed Rilke's attention like a sponge, and allowed him no time to moon about the state of his soul. The Duse, aging, off the boards and out of limelight, was struggling to keep an actor and hopeful impresario, Alexander Moissi, as well as a young playwright, Lina Poletti, in her weakening orbit. Rilke perceived the relation between the young woman and the Duse as one which resembled his own unhappy service with Rodin, and the actress's plight a forecast for the poet's aging self. Caught in her storms, he rocked from side to side, only, ultimately, to be marooned. The triangle dissolved, and Rilke fell back into his own.

After a series of séances arranged by the princess (too embarrassing to sane minds to be described here), Rilke's spirit was beckoned to Spain by the spirit of the *planchette*. Nonetheless, the country the poet sought existed only in the paintings of El Greco, which contained angels worthy of the *Elegies*, nor did Toledo, seen through such a framer as the painter, disappoint. One night, standing on one of the bridges that spans the Tagus, Rilke watched a meteor sear the dark sky, and retained its image for several poems. Were the *Elegies* to arrive in a brightness like the meteor's, only to burn up in the blaze of their own being?

"The Spanish Trilogy," three of the finest poems he managed during the Great Ten-Year Drought (which wasn't so dry after all), were written in the following January at Ronda. The first of these poems is particularly extraordinary because, for all of Rilke's orality, he rarely imposes on a poem a purely rhetorical order. He will often adopt a dramatic form, and speak from a particular point of view—a beggar's, a blind man's, and so on—but he is only occasionally the orator. This prayer—for that is what it is, a desperate prayer—we listen to, but we cannot, could not, utter. Prayers are too personal. We overhear.

> From this cloud—look!—which has so stormily hid
> the star that just now shone there—(and from me),
> from this dark huddle of hills which holds the night,
> the night-winds, for a while—(and from me),
> from this valley's stream which reshines
> the tumult of the night sky—(and from me);
> from me, and all of this, to make, Lord,
> some single thing: from me and the feeling
> with which the herd, penned in its stalls,
> accepts with a long slow sigh
> the darkening departure of the world—
> from me and every glimmer of light
> amid the dimness of many houses, Lord:
> to make one thing; from strangers,
> since I know not one, Lord, and from me, from me,
> to make *one* thing; from the sleepers,
> those bereft old men in the hospice
> who, with importance, cough in bed,
> from children sleepdrunk on the breasts of strangers,
> from so much that's uncertain, and always from me,
> from me alone and all I don't know,
> to make the Thing, Lord Lord Lord, the Thing
> that, both earthly and cosmic like a meteor,
> takes for its heaviness only the sum of its flight,
> to weigh nothing but arrival.[4]

With the artistic and physical geography in place, with his stand-up desk and a tiled stove delivered, with housewarming Christmas gifts of chandeliers and lamps from friends, Rilke can write a few letters to his lady loves (it is difficult not to become caustic)—to Clara, to his daughter, Ruth, to Nanny Wunderly-Volkart, to Lou Salomé, Baladine Klossowska—yes, to his new love called Merline now, or Mouky in private—and almost by the way, to Gertrud Ouckama Knoop, informing her of his daughter's forthcoming marriage, inasmuch as she and Gertrud Knoop's daughter Wera had once been friends. Wera, who had hoped to become a dancer, had fallen ill of leukemia and died at 19, two years before. Now Rilke chooses to console the mother, and an exchange of letters ensues, leading to another gift: the diary Wera had kept during her painful months of dying. A dying which her diary will, for Rilke, ironically forecast.

If things constantly come into being only to pass away, patterns nevertheless persist and appear and reappear with remarkable frequency and stubbornness. In 1913, Rilke acknowledges the receipt of a copy of Paula Becker's diary, sent to him by her brother, informing him of what his "Requiem" for her had already said: that this was the death which had shaken him more than any other.

The death of a beautiful young woman—it was Edgar Allan Poe's opinion—was the best choice for a great poem's appropriately poetic subject. Certainly such a death—its tragic yet uplifting meaning—had obsessed Rilke during nearly his entire life. Not only did it seem that a girl had to die to make room in the world for him, but it also seemed that this otherwise sad prematurity preserved the child's possibilities along with her innocence. Victimized by death, she could not be victimized by life. The stoicism which made up a great part of Rilke's moral character also glorified, for him, acts of relinquishment and asceticism. Lovers who loved and lost but who continued more devotedly to love, like Gaspara Stampa (an Italian noblewoman who composed two hundred sonnets to commemorate her unhappy passion) were his sort of saint. These were the sentimental reasons. Rilke's jilted ladies (and all were left in some sort of lurch) ought to love him the more for his resistance. And they did.

Baladine Klossowska, the painter with whom the poet had conjugated at Muzot for a few weeks before winter's onset, had thumbtacked a postcard reproduction of Orpheus, sitting under a tree surrounded by tamely attentive wild animals, above Rilke's writing desk. Furthermore, Rilke had just completed his translation of Michelangelo's sonnets and was thinking about experimenting with the form. All the requisite elements were assembled. On February 2, he began a few of them, dedicated to the memory of a young woman he had scarcely known (just as earlier he had written a requiem for a poet, Count Wolf von Kalckreuth, whom he had never met). Wera had become a musician by force of fatal circumstance, so that the choice of Orpheus was certainly appropriate. As if he were hearing another voice, there, suddenly, the words were: *Da stieg ein Baum*. And they weighed nothing but arrival. The storm had begun.

"What is the cause that, among the thousand products of our unconscious activity, some are called to pass the threshold, while others remain below?" Poincaré asks. His answer is significant, I think, and sound.

More generally the privileged unconscious phenomena, those susceptible of becoming conscious, are those which, directly or indirectly, affect most profoundly our emotional sensibility.

We may associate mathematical work solely with the intellect,

but this would be to forget the feeling of mathematical beauty, of the harmony of numbers and forms, of geometric elegance. This is a true esthetic feeling that all real mathematicians know.

Of course we cannot ignore the differences between mathematical discoveries and poetic connections, because mathematical problems are well-defined and specific (for the most part), whereas poems can seem to pop up like toast from an empty toaster. Moreover, the mathematician is uncovering laws which are already there; they exist in the realm of number, where the pioneer, like a verdant valley, finds them. Making and finding are fundamentally different. Nor should we make light of the gap between the preestablished and formal character of Rilke's recently practiced sonnet, and the loosely shaped and individual nature of his *Elegies*. Yet in Rilke's case these differences are diminished. In a sense the *Elegies* were there waiting, too. Whole pieces were present, and fragments suggested the true shapes of the other jars. Rilke had written them over and over already. There is scarcely a line, an image, an idea, that we cannot find, slightly rearranged, in earlier work.

Better than almost any other poet, Rilke understood that relations between elements, not the elements themselves, were at the heart of any art, and that these relations made up its "space," and were the source of a poem's "geometry." "What are the mathematic entities to which we attribute this character of beauty and elegance, and which are capable of developing in us a sort of esthetic emotion?" Poincaré asks. And answers: "They are those whose elements are harmoniously disposed so that the mind without effort can embrace their totality while realizing the details."[5]

Mathematical and other conceptual blockages are often the result of the thinker's remaining with a strategy or set of similar strategies to which he seems wedded. He needs to start off in a fresh direction, but is unable because most first efforts form a track into which the pencil-end of the mind slips, over and over. Hence the helpfulness of the distraction. It allows another idea to appear. I do not believe the completion of the *Elegies* was delayed for a decade for purely poetic reasons. I suspect that Rilke, first of all, could not satisfactorily fill out his metaphysics, and second, could not find the language which would provide that metaphysics with its justification, and third, was not yet the poet to whom the work could be revealed.

The *Elegies* were to provide us with a comprehensive outlook or attitude toward the world and in particular the poet's role in it. We should not ennoble ideas that are made mostly of emotions, moods, and attitudes by calling them philosophical. Nor were they at all religious despite the presence (or absence, actually) of the Angels. The *Elegies* present us with conclusions, not arguments, so—again—they cannot be philosophical. And they are not revelations supported by a Faith. Their justification—their proof—is poetical and lies in the persuasive power of the language they arrive in. If Rilke could not resolve the oppositions which were everywhere in evidence in his outlook, he could not find the language which would allow him to affirm a solution. In short, he had not yet found the right metaphors; or, in those cases where he had them, he had not yet reached their inner nature.

In the first poem of "The Spanish Trilogy," he had asked in anguish to be allowed, just once, in just one thing, to achieve the unity of the world with himself: from me, from me, Lord. In a poem called "The Great [or perhaps Vast] Night," written a year later, in the Paris to which he had returned, the earlier alienation is expressed again, now not in a petition, but in a statement of fact. The poem's beginning is startling. It suggests that the window represents a larger, more spiritual opening.

Often I gazed at you in wonder, stood at the window
I started the day before, stood and gazed at you in wonder.
The new city still seemed to warn me away,
and the recalcitrant landscape darkened
as if I weren't there. Even things close by
didn't care if I didn't understand them. The street
leapt to the top of the lamppost. I saw how strange it was.
Over there—a room, empathetic, lit by its lantern—
I'd begin to take part; they'd notice, clap shut the shutters.
I stood. And then a child cried. I knew what the mothers
in the surrounding houses could do—
and the inconsolable source of all sorrow.
Or a voice sang, exceeding expectations,
or downstairs an old man coughed reproachfully,
as if his body had it right and the gentle world was wrong.
Then an hour was struck, but I began to count too late
and it got by me. —Like a new boy at school,
when he's finally allowed to join in,
who can't catch the ball, and is a bumbler
at all the games the others play so easily,
so he just stands there and stares—where?—
I stood, and suddenly saw that *you* had befriended me,
played with me now, grown-up Night, and I gazed
at you in wonder. While towers threatened,
while the city surrounded me, its aims still a secret,

and unfathomable mountains pitched their camp against me,
and strangeness prowled in tightening circles
around the random fires my senses set—it was then,
great Night, you weren't ashamed to know me.
Your breath passed over me. Across all those solemn
spaces, your smile spread to enter me.[6]

Now Rilke knew what the glue was.

SCHADE

One might sentimentally imagine that Rilke's separation from his wife, Clara, or his break with Rodin, especially his rejection by Lou, would be decisive in his life. Certainly, the onset of the *Elegies* was one such stroke, and not altogether salutary in its character either. Taking a more prosaic tack, one could be practical and suggest that the surprising popularity of his youthful prose poem *The Lay of the Love and Death of the Cornet Christoph Rilke*, which furnished him a much-needed income after it was published in a cheap pocket-size edition in 1912, was very significant. The dismal early Paris days were critical. World War I threw Rilke into a profound and enduring gloom—for both personal and humanitarian reasons. That might reach the Top Ten. In lives, it is hard to measure such things. Vital factors are sneaky and, like our internal organs, do most of their work out of sight. With Rilke, however, I think we always need to accept the cliché and *cherchez la femme*. So near the head of such a list, however suspect such lists of wounds and awards are, I should want to place the death of Paula Modersohn-Becker, the blond painter of Rilke's Worpswede journal.

In the early days of his acquaintance with the colony's artists, it is fairly obvious that Rilke was most taken by Paula Becker, and that she responded to his interest is also clear; but Paula had grown close to Otto Modersohn as he waited out his wife's death through a lengthy illness. He was a painter of some reputation, mostly for work in a style that was called Naturlyrismus, which aimed at not only the adoration of Nature but the veneration of the peasant whose relation to the soil was simple, noble, and direct. Modersohn's sentiments and Rilke's Russian boots and tunic would find much to talk about. As a suitor, Modersohn got several things right: he was enthusiastic about Paula's paintings, which few others were; he found her attitude toward art admirable; and he thought that her personality—"charming, sweet, strong, healthy, energetic"—filled in the blanks in his own. Had Rilke wished to woo her, he'd have gotten off on the wrong foot, for he took no notice of her work, nor did he discuss either Paula or Clara in his Worpswede monograph.

Older, established, with a manner some called "magisterial," Modersohn's greatest advantage was the sympathy his ailing wife could elicit for him. In any case, Paula soon, and rather passively, it appears, found herself framed for marriage. Since her middle-class Bremen family was urging her to find a position as a governess, she may have thought that marriage to a painter would be a good escape. She'd have a husband knowledgeable about, and sympathetic with, her aims. To his credit, Modersohn did sincerely encourage and support his wife's work, but Paula confesses to her diary how little understanding from him she feels she has, and how frequently she weeps. Marriage, she writes, does not make one happier. And now Worpswede is no longer a cozy enclosure. She pines for Paris. From 1903 to 1907 she will make three trips—lasting a month, several months, finally a year. Marriage did not make her happy. Paris did.

Because Paula found it increasingly irritating to have Modersohn's tutorial eye still following her brush, blocking her way more and more often with cautionary words; and because, at some indeterminate point, she realized that her husband was mediocre and could not lay claim to artistic superiority; because, as a woman, no one expected much of her as an artist; because when she showed her work, it was castigated; because when she painted, she felt she entered her real self; because, as pleasantly vibrant in society as Paula appeared, she was sensitive and shy by nature; because ordinary hausfrau life left her deeply unsatisfied and bored; because . . . From however many causes, for however many reasons, she became an artistic loner, painting in private and for herself, so much so that after her death, when Heinrich Vogeler and her husband entered her studio, they were surprised to find "a wealth of work" of whose existence they had been unaware.

Because . . . Clara had become so absorbed in her wifely, motherly life, she had no room in the arms of her intimacy for her formerly close friend, and in a letter Paula complained of the way "the old gang" (as the song says) had been broken up. It was Rilke who wrote back to Frau Modersohn ("exuding oily didacticism," as Freedman says),[1] suggesting that the Rilkes had reached a higher plane.

Actually, the couple's plane had crashed, and they were scattered about like baggage on incongenial ground. Later, after Rilke and Clara had rid themselves of Ruth and established themselves in Paris, Paula came to visit, but the once happy trio couldn't play well together anymore, and Paula found both of them—sewn like button to sleeve—to be bores. Even though Paula's work was slowly seeping into him, Rilke was painfully preoccupied with Rodin, with the unsteady state of his marriage, with the alienation and self-doubt that would fever *Malte* and pave its pages with exquisite gloom and pain. About this time—the poet could not have failed to perceive it—Paula's formerly high opinion of him sank out of sight in the sea of narcissism she felt now enveloped him. Both fled the city in the same week.

Three years later, in 1906, they met again in Paris. This time Rilke was breaking up with Rodin, and Becker had officially left her husband. They got on better now. Paula was at her best, painting odd nude portraits of herself. One in particular impressed the poet. Called *Self-Portrait on Her Sixth Wedding Day,* it has a background of pale splotchy wallpaper, and shows Paula, naked to just below the waist, standing slightly sideways and looking askance. The faces she was making at this time were becoming more and more Coptic. Hanging around her neck and falling between her breasts is a necklace of fat amber beads. The beads will show up in a much happier, even finer portrait from the same year. In the *Wedding Day* painting, the colors are washed out and, prophetically, Paula's belly swells with her future fate; but in the later one her characteristic earth tones return, she becomes a Gauguin native, her lower lip is thick and red, she is holding flowers, there are flowers in her hair and flowers in an Henri Rousseau background of tall leafy stems.

She painted tomatoes, chestnuts, several still lifes with pottery jugs, and fruit in the spirit of Cézanne—a plate of apples sitting beside a green glass. The painter and the poet would meet for dinner at some vegetarian restaurant Rilke had selected, hoping that the asparagus would be delicate and plump, the tips tender. Paula began a painting of her friend at about the same time Rilke was writing his own "Self-Portrait from the Year 1906."[2] The background that fills hers is olive drab, the paint thick throughout—paint in which a pallet knife leaves marks like icing tracks. Rilke wears his hair in a cap, and his Fu Manchu mustache, his goatee, his spade-shaped beard, are as brown as his hair, his shoulders, and his featureless eyes—featureless except for wide red rims which circle them like orbits that hopefully continue to spin although their planets have long ago left them. In both poem and painting the mouth is "made as a mouth is, wide and straight," but in Becker's painting the jaw has dropped, the mouth gapes. The pink-rimmed eyes, the pink ears, pink lips, are a Paula Becker trademark. Her figures have grown blocky and brown and worn—worn because the surface of the paint has become streaked and flaky, the colors faded, like the side of an old barn.

From Worpswede calls came which were not satisfactorily answered, so Otto Modersohn, the husband who was supporting his wife in her separation from him, arrives to implore her to return. Paula's refusal to leave Paris, her insistence on divorce, frightened Rilke, who stopped sitting for his portrait and ducked—as if guilty of some indiscretion—out of sight. The painting remains as unfinished as his self-portrait poem suggests his great work was. Nevertheless, it is boldly signed PMB, the M in the middle still like a river between towns. As long as Paula stayed tied to Modersohn the poet felt safe, and he bound himself to Clara, in a similarly loose yet protective way. Neither could drift off. But now he began to put his customary distance between them.

Rilke, as if he were Achilles in Zeno's famous race, will grow nearer to each of the women he fancies, reducing the difference to a hair's width, so long as there remains a space no spark can jump; so if Paula is going to declare to Otto: "I don't want you as my husband," and "I don't want any child from you," then Rilke will stay clear of her company;[3] but when, pressured by her husband, family, and friends, she reconciles, and the couple's return to Worpswede is announced, Rilke reappears full of warm regard, with photos from his latest journey and an inscribed copy of *Book of Pictures*, his most recent publication.

If the person of the poet has betrayed his friend, the poet has betrayed his principles. Because he knew . . . he knew Paula's situation. He should have supported her separation. But no one—not even Paula's sister, Herma, whom she loved—not even her friend Clara, whom she'd counted on—no one—no one—did.

Most women in Rilke's day, unless they were barren or rich, were married off early and sent into a life of loveless broodmaring that led, after an interval that demonstrated their decency, to the bearing, the nursing, the raising, and the burying of children—six, eight, ten—losing their health and figure in the bargain, as well as any chance at achievement. Paula felt the attractions of motherhood, and painted satisfied babies at satisfying bosoms, and children, too, with awe and warmth. But, in addition to the down payment on the child's life you were making—how many years would each cost, and bluntly, how many paintings?—when you gave birth, you courted Death, who often said, "Come with me." Had not Paula Becker, relinquishing her art to perform a customary social service, cast away her vocation? Had she not allowed her husband's lesser talent to dominate and destroy hers? The family may have felt like a fist to Rilke, but its grip kept women home. It held them down and hit them often.

Ultimately, money settled the matter. How would Paula live if Modersohn didn't support her? She had no training in anything but art; the social status of unwealthy divorced women was shaky; job opportunities for them were few and unscheduled; Paris was expensive (compared to Worpswede); and success for a female in her field was unlikely indeed. The situation forced an accommodation. Economics was the other fist.

Reconciliations have their own momentum. Giving up always goes beyond the given that has been intended. Paula became pregnant during the March of Modersohn's arrival in Paris, and gifted her husband with a daughter, Mathilde, on the 2nd of November 1907. It hadn't been that easy, but a prolonged rest was regularly prescribed. The new mother (and now the madonna of the restored family) was to be bedridden until the 20th.

Paula Becker had always believed her life would be a short one. As early as July of 1900, she writes in her diary:

> Worpswede, July 26, 1900
>
> As I was painting today, some thoughts came to me and I want to write them down for the people I love. I know I shall not live very long. But I wonder, is that sad? Is a celebration more beautiful because it lasts longer? And my life is a celebration, a short, intense celebration. My powers of perception are becoming finer, as if I were supposed to absorb everything in the few years that are still to be offered me, everything. My sense of smell is unbelievably keen at present. With almost every breath I take, I get a new sense and understanding of the linden tree, of ripened wheat, of hay, and of mignonette. I suck everything up into me. And if only now love would blossom for me, before I depart; and if I can paint three good pictures, then I shall go gladly, with flowers in my hair.[4]

After three weeks, Paula Becker gets out of bed for the first time. Crowned by freshly combed and braided hair, with roses pinned to her dressing gown, she walks slowly from her bedroom, flanked by her husband and her brother in case she should suffer a sudden weakness, into another room, where dozens of candles have been lit and placed about.

> You sat up in your childbed
> to confront a mirror that gave back everything.
> Now that image was all of you, *out there*,

> inside was mere deception, the sweet deceit
> of every woman who tries a smile while
> she puts on her jewelry and combs her hair.[5]

Seated in a chair, she asks for her baby to be brought to her. This is done. "Now it is almost as beautiful as Christmas." She tries to elevate her foot, perhaps to place it on a footstool. And dies then of an embolism. It's said she said *Schade!*"—what a shame.

A year later, after the death of the Countess von Schwerin, too, and then, suddenly of typhoid fever, his Capri hostess, Alice Faehndrich—in short, with death the atmosphere—Rilke wrote a requiem to a woman he would not name. Unnamed even on her monument, I suspect, because Otto Modersohn was, of course, still alive, still there to be hurt, still there to take umbrage at what the work would say. Almost the moment Paula's poem was completed, Rilke wrote another requiem, this one for a suicide he'd never personally known, Count Wolf von Kalckreuth, but in this case the identity of the dead is prominently displayed.

Paula Becker's stock as an artist has risen some over the years, but at the time (though one thinks the thought wryly and without vainglory) those who knew her had to believe that the climax of her brief life was the death which occasioned the composition of Rilke's "Requiem for a Friend," one of poetry's eternal triumphs.

"I've had my dead, and I let them go," it begins, "and was surprised to see them so consoled, so soon at home in being dead, so right, so unlike their reputation." (The *Elegies* will argue otherwise, deciding that "it's difficult to be dead.") Only Paula Becker assumes the mantle of the traditional restless spirit and continues to trouble her friend. What is the point of coming back from the dead if it's only to visit the dead, because everything in this so-called life disappears in the very moment of its brief appearance?

Bitterly, the poet promises to do the things, see the things, feel the things which the painter didn't live to enjoy; bitterly he blames her for acceding to custom, abandoning her art, dying a death designed and demanded by an undeserving society, a system she should have opposed; bitterly he accuses her of eating the seeds of her own death, bending her own path from its true course, upending, as if it were an enemy, her proper end; and now she has rejected her death as well, to return, to beg for something from the life she left which can no more be given her; bitterly the poem accuses, not Modersohn alone, not merely Rainer Maria Rilke (who hides now behind the universal), but Men in general for Paula's premature departure. The social condition in which women find themselves is partly to blame, but the opposition between life and art which society also insists on is a considerable factor. Love demands an increase of freedom for one's lover, and justice asks that we measure it by the amount we command in ourselves.

"Don't come back," the poem ends. Later, Rilke will issue the same command to Orpheus: remain with Eurydice in the realm of the dead. "If you can stand it, stay dead with the dead, the dead have their own concerns." No longer bitterly, but with a resignation which does not relieve him of his obligations, the poet promises to carry on the task she should have stayed here to perform, but now he asks for her help, if she must come back at all, and if it won't distract her from her new responsibilities, "since, in me, what is most distant sometimes helps." The final line, in German, is even more revealing:

> Doch hilf mir so, dass es dich nicht zerstreut,
> wie mird das Fernste manchmal hilft: in mir.

That *in mir*, placed as it is at the end of both line and poem (and creating, for any English version, an intolerable awkwardness), suspends the entire text behind the colon, and makes (as is customary with Rilke) the poem even more deeply personal.

Paula Becker's ghost remained at large to trouble the poet despite his poem's pleas. A selection from Paula's journals had been assembled by her brother, Kurt, and published in a magazine, *Güldenkammer*, in 1913. Rilke had read these pieces and was sufficiently impressed to suggest to their editor that all of Paula's manuscripts should be made available. We should not cry out, "Lo, and behold," when, in the autumn of 1916, Paula's mother sent a packet of her daughter's journals and letters to Rilke, requesting that he edit them and see to their publication, because people were always sending such intimacies to him, and would again. Rilke had written his own Florence and Schmargendorf diaries for Lou Salomé's eyes. The practice was common.

On this occasion, however, after a delay that extends to the day after Christmas, and in a lengthy letter which squirms like a worm, Rilke refuses Frau Becker's request, and repeatedly insists that these letters and journals (picked over and selected by the family to be sure) do not do Paula Becker's achievement justice, because most of them reflect her earlier views and the level of her early work, whereas the painting she did in her final Paris period, which establishes and defines her genius, is inadequately reflected by the written materials that Rilke has in hand.

Whenever one evokes the name of Paula Becker, one has implicitly to assert that in the power of her later work she produced an extraordinarily personal style, and one will never come closer to this "personal" essence than by realizing that it resides in that most astonishing tension between validity and grace. For precisely in the middle, between a validity already remote from her and a newly entered state of liveliness, already grown modest, there stands and endures her pure, free, sacrificial achievement.[6]

These sentences are stuffed with phrases of postponement and evasion, just as the entire letter is. Yet Rilke may have been right. There is no better hiding place than behind the truth. Who will part that drape?

When the publisher Anton Kippenberg accepts the editorial task that Rilke has refused, the poet writes, opposing the project for the same reasons he has earlier advanced: that such a volume would tarnish rather than enhance her reputation: "It may simply be that her final years were too short to permit any articulation whatsoever alongside the breathless progress of her art . . ."[7]

What is most distant sometimes helps. Many years later, when the critic Hermann Pongs, in a questionnaire about the *Elegies* which became a major source for their understanding, asked Rilke for his impression of Paula Becker's late paintings, he shamefully answered, "I last saw Paula Modersohn in Paris in 1906 and knew little of the work she was doing then or later— *work I don't know to this day.*"[8]

If guilt can write a great poem, it's been accomplished here, for Rilke also brought his own wife to bed with child. That had to be borne upon him—his resemblance to Modersohn. He did so despite the fact that he felt (somewhat inconsistently) that children supplanted in women the need for creativity. Clara survived her pregnancy, yet soon had the burden of a baby and another's life to manage all alone . . . yes, alas, since her husband, having become bourgeois, as Paula was to, and having succumbed to custom, as Paula would (even if Clara had begged—as, later, Modersohn must have—for a child) . . . had then—against all the poet's aims and principles—inseminated the woman he said he loved, the artist he claimed to admire, thus endangering her life (as Modersohn would Paula's) . . . and again, when finally, attempting to escape the consequences of that crime, he finds he faces yet others—principally the couple's joint entrapment in common life—he selfishly flees his new family, seeks refuge in Rodin, suffers as a substitute the poverties of Paris . . . yes . . . well . . . alas . . . but these were actions and attitudes which redoubled his guilt, troubled his conscience, and disturbed his sleep, because the poet's very real very sordid very ordinary weaknesses were always threatening to appear before the fair public figure of the Poet Personified, take its place, and, as he said he feared Paula's journals would, disgrace the work of a life.

Under her changed and straitened circumstances Clara could only hope to continue with her sculpture. But hope is the lone evil those evils left behind when they popped out of Pandora's box. For how much of Clara's imitation of her husband—leaving her child as he had both of them—must the husband accept responsibility, having set the tone and led the way?

Toward Paula, too, at the end, the poet had been ambivalent, unhelpful, distant—quadrupling the counts against him. As with most apparitions, guilt is the ghost that walks within the "Requiem." Whenever a poem of Rilke's seems to admonish its reader, openly with "You must change your life," or tacitly, through the poem's example, we can be certain that Rilke himself has failed the charge.

REQUIEM FOR A FRIEND

I've had my dead, and I let them go
and was surprised to see them so consoled,
so soon at home in being dead, so right,
so unlike their reputation. Only you,
you come back, brush by me, move about,
bump into something that will betray
your presence with a sound. Oh, don't take
from me what I was slowly learning. You're mistaken
if you feel homesick for anything here.
We alter all of it; whatever we perceive
is instantly reflected from ourselves,
and is no longer there.

I thought you were farther off. It bothers
me that you should stray and come this way,
you who managed more transformation than any other woman.
That we were frightened by your death—no . . .
that your harsh death darkly interrupted us,
dividing what-had-been from what-would-be:
this is our concern; coming to terms with it
will accompany all our tasks.
But that you too were frightened, and even now
tremble with terror when terror has no cause;
that you are giving up some of your eternity
to return here, friend, here again,
where nothing yet *is*; that, half-hearted
and confused by your first encounter with Totality,
you did not follow the unfolding of infinite natures,
as once you grasped earthly things;
that, from the circle that received you,

the stubborn pull of some past discontent
has dragged you back into calibrated time—
this starts me from sleep like the break-in of a thief.
If I could say that you only come out of your
abundant kindness, that because you are so sure
and self-possessed you can wander childlike here and there,
unaware of any risk from harmful places—
but no: you're beseeching. That's what chills me
to the bone and cuts me like a saw.
A grim rebuke, borne to me by your ghost,
might weigh on me at night when I withdraw
into my lungs, my guts,
into the emptied chambers of my heart—
such a protest would not be as grotesque
as this pleading is. What do you want?

 Tell me, should I travel? Did you leave some
Thing behind that runs after you now in vain?
Should I set out for a country you never saw,
though it was the other half of all you knew?

 I shall sail its rivers, search its earth, and ask
about its oldest customs, speaking with women in
      their doorways,
and watching when they call their children home.
I shall see how they wrap their world around them
when they work the fields and graze their meadows.
I shall ask to be brought before their king,
and bribe the priests to take me to their temple,
so I may prostrate myself before their most powerful idol,
and have them leave me there, after latching the gates.
But then, when I have learned enough,
I shall simply watch the animals until
something of their serenity slowly
seeps into my limbs; I shall see myself

held deep inside their eyes until gradually,
calmly, indifferently, I'm released.
I shall have gardeners recite to me
the many flowers so I can bring back
in the pots of their proper names
some trace of a hundred scents.
And I shall buy fruits, too, fruits in whose juice
a country's earth will rise to join its sky.

  For fruit you understood: ripe fruits.
You set them out in bowls before you,
and on a scale of colors weighed their worth.
You saw women, too, as fruit; children as well,
since they grew the shapes of their existence
as if from a seed inside.
And finally you saw yourself so—as a fruit.
Peeling from your clothes, you brought
your nakedness before a mirror,
and waded in up to your gaze, which stayed wide-eyed,
in front, and did not say: I'm that; no: *this is*.
You looked with such a lack of curiosity,
so impersonally and with the poverty of the pure,
you weren't attracted even by yourself: now holy.

  I'd like to keep you where you put yourself—
in the deeps of the mirror, away from the world.
Why have you come in this different way?
Why do you deny yourself? Why do you want
to make me think that in the amber beads
you wore in your portrait there was still
a heaviness of the sort that can't survive
in the serenity of peaceful pictures? Why does
your posture seem to show an evil omen?
What makes you read the contours of your body
like lines on the palm of a hand,

so that I cannot see them otherwise than Fate?
   Come into the candlelight. I'm not afraid
to look the dead in the face. When they come back
they have a right, as much as other things,
to the hospitality of our gaze.
   Come; we'll be together silent for a while.
Look at this rose on my writing desk:
isn't the light around it just as shy
as that which shines around you? It too has no business here.
It ought to have bloomed or perished in the garden
out there quite apart from me,
yet here it is, unaware of my awareness.

Don't be frightened if I finally understand,
for—oh!—I feel it rising in me; I can do nothing else,
I must grasp and grant it, even if I die in doing so.
I must concede that you are here.
Just as a blind man touches something,
I feel your Fate, although I cannot name it.
Let us grieve together that someone
withdrew you from your mirror. Can you still cry?
You can't. Long ago you turned the strength and abundance of
     your tears
into a richly ripe gaze, and were transforming
everything vital that was flowing in you
into a more powerful reality—
rising and circling, poised but wild.
Then chance drew you back, utmost chance
drew you back from the last step needed to advance,
back into a world where the body's blood rules.
Not all of you at once, but bit by bit;
but when, around these bits, the world,
like pus around a wound, grew,

then you needed the whole self you no longer had,
and, against the rules, broke yourself further, fell into painful
    fragments,
as you had to, because you so needed *you*.
Then, bearing yourself away, you grubbed
from your nightwarm heartsoil the green seeds
from which your death was meant to sprout:
yours, your own death, the proper outcome of your life.
And you ate, you ate the kernels of your own death
as you would eat any grain, ate them all,
to find an aftertaste of sweetness
you hadn't expected, lurking, a sweetness on your lips,
you: who inside the sensations of your senses
were so sweet already.

    Ah . . . let us lament. Do you know with what hesitation,
what reluctance, your blood, when you called it back,
gave up its commitment to an incomparable circulation?
how confused it became when asked to take up
once again the restricted circuits of the body?
how, full of mistrust and astonishment, it flowed
into the placenta again, exhausted suddenly
from the long journey home?
You drove it on, you pushed it ahead,
you dragged it to the hearth like a herd to be sacrificed,
and wanted it, despite all that, to be happy.
Finally you conquered: it *was* happy;
it showed a flag and surrendered. You believed,
because you'd got used to those other measures,
that it would remain only for a time.
But now you were *in* time, and time is long.
And time goes on, and time adds up, and time
is like a relapse after a lengthy illness.

    How short your life seems if you now compare it

with the hours you sat before your overflowing art
and its overflowing future, diverting their course
to stir the seed that would become your child,
and, once again, your Fate. A bitter business.
Labor exceeding strength. Yet you performed it.
Day after day you dragged yourself to the loom
and pulled out its lovely work and rewove
its threads into another pattern.
And still had energy enough for a celebration.

When it was done you wanted to be rewarded,
like children who've drunk the bittersweet tea
that was supposed to make them well.
So you rewarded yourself, since you were still
so far away from everyone, even after this, that no one
could have guessed what reward would please.
But you knew. You sat up in your childbed
to confront a mirror that gave back everything.
Now that image was all of you, *out there*,
inside was mere deception, the sweet deceit
of every woman who tries a smile while
she puts on her jewelry and combs her hair.

And so you died as women used to die,
died in your own warm house,
died the old-fashioned death of childbearing women
who try to close themselves again but cannot do it,
because that darkness that they also bore
comes back again and bullies its way in like a callous lover.

Even so, shouldn't someone have rounded up
a few wailing-women. Women who will weep for money,
and if well paid will howl for you all night,
when otherwise all is quiet.
Customs! We haven't nearly enough customs.
All gone and out of use.

Reading Rilke

So that's what you had to come back for:
the mourning that was omitted. Do you hear mine?
I should like to clothe you in my cries,
cover the sharp shatters of your death,
and tug till the cloth is all in rags, so my poor words
would have to shuffle around
shivering in the tatters of their sound—
as if lamentation were enough. But now I accuse:
not the one who withdrew you from yourself
(I cannot find him hereabouts, he looks like all the others),
but through him I accuse . . . I accuse all men.

If, from somewhere deep inside me,
there were to arise a childlife I hadn't been aware of,
perhaps the purest childness of my childhood,
I wouldn't want to know it. Without looking,
I'd make an angel of it, hurl it into the front row
of those weeping angels who remember God.

For this sort of suffering has gone on long enough;
and no one's learned to bear it; it's too hard for us,
the insane suffering of spurious love
that, upheld by the precepts of custom,
calls itself Right and prospers from the Wrong.
Where is the man with the rights of such possession,
who can control what cannot even possess itself,
but will now and then happily catch hold,
only to toss itself away again like a child's ball?
As little as a captain can keep the carved Nike
facing forward from his ship's prow
when the inner lightness of her divinity
whisks her away on a wave of wind;
so little can one of us call back the woman
who, now no longer heeding us, sets forth
on the wire-thin strip of her existence

without a misstep, as if by a miracle—
unless our pleasure and profession is to wrong.
　For *this* is wrong, if anything is wrong:
not to increase the freedom of a love
with all the inner freedom one can muster.
We have, where we love, only this:
we must allow each other to grow great, because diminishing
comes easily to us and doesn't need to be learned.

　Are you still there? In what corner are you?
You understood so much, you did so much;
You passed through life as open as daybreak.
Women suffer; loving is lonely;
and artists in their work sometimes sense,
where they love, the need for transmutation.
You began both; both live in that
which fame distorts by taking it away.
Oh, you were far from all fame. You were
inconspicuous; had gently withdrawn your beauty
as one lowers a festive flag
on the gray morning of a working day.
You had but one wish, for a lifetime of work—
which is not done: despite all, not done.
　If you're still there, if there is still a place
in this darkness where your spirit resonates
with the shallow soundwaves that a voice,
by itself, in the night, stirs up in the air of a lofty room:
hear me; help me. Look, we inadvertently
slip back from what we've labored to attain
into routines we never intended, where
we weakly struggle, as in a dream, and die there
without ever waking. No one will be any wiser.
Anyone who has lifted his heart for a lengthy task

may discover that he can't keep on, the weight
of the work is too great, so it falls of that weight, worthless.
For somewhere there's an ancient enmity
between ordinary life and extraordinary work.
To understand, to express it: help me.
    Don't come back. If you can bear it, stay
dead among the dead. The dead have their own concerns.
But help me, if you can, if it won't distract you,
since—in me—what is most distant sometimes helps.[9]

THE GRACE OF GREAT THINGS

In 1919, at summer's end, while staying in the Swiss town of Soglio, where he was given access to the library of the Palazzo Salis and was able to acquaint himself there with some of the Salis family past (it was Rilke's habit to look into the background of the families and the houses in which he became a guest), Rilke allowed his mind to drift back to those allegedly hideous days in the Military School of St. Pölten, and to an inventive physics teacher who one day set up an experiment to teach his pupils a few things about the nature of sound. The essay inspired by this memory is one of the strangest and most revealing of his pieces, and Rilke liked it well enough to include it as a sample of his prose when he gave public readings from his works—at Winterthur, for instance.

At their instructor's direction, the young *bricoleurs* found a piece of pliable cardboard, which they twisted into the shape of a funnel. Over the narrow end they fastened a piece of wax-like paper normally used to close up fruit jars. This was to be the vibrating membrane into whose center they thrust a clothes-brush bristle. A small cylinder about the size of a typewriter platen, I imagine, and equipped with a rotating handle was then coated with candle wax and brought in contact with the bristle. When someone spoke into the funnel, the bristle bristled, scratching the wax on the slowly turning cylinder. The exact character of its course, Rilke remembers, was preserved by a coat of varnish.

Miraculously, as it must have seemed, when the needle retraced its previous path, "the sound which had been ours," Rilke writes, "came back to us tremblingly, haltingly from the paper funnel, uncertain, infinitely soft and hesitating and fading out altogether in places." He thought he would remember that tremulous whisper forever, but what really remained in his mind were the grooves on the cylinder. The lesson Rilke learned should be of immeasurable importance to all of us. Wittgenstein would later use the relations among the musical score, the performance, and the phonograph to express a similar point. Rilke had heard, then seen, how a few spoken words could be transformed (one of his talismanic terms) into a modest physical groove—a line—which so preserved those sounds that they could be recovered again. The matter was, of course, more complex than that. Movements in a larynx had set the air to vibrating. The vibrations in the air became vibrations in the membrane and hence wiggles in the bristle, which wrote them upon the slowly revolving wax.

This process—of transforming and detransforming a sound into a groove and back again—was possible because both media passed the form along; that is, the media retained the relations, although they expressed them differently. Galileo, as if he were the most divine of magicians, represented a moving body as a point, the time and distance of its travel as vectors from which a rectangle might be constructed. The formula for the distance traveled at a certain speed over a fixed time was identical with the formula for the area of a rectangle: $a = xy$, or $d = vt$. When Descartes discovered analytic geometry, he transformed geometry into algebra, and mechanics was consequently also drawn into algebra's abstractness. There are two kinds of transformations, then: material (vibration of the brush into wiggles of the groove) and conceptual (geometry elevated into algebra). It was a move of this conceptual sort that Poincaré had performed.

Rilke regularly achieved such conceptual elevations in his poems by having one metaphor set upon, swallow, and digest another. And then another . . . like the traditional line of increasingly large-mouthed and voracious fish.

Many years later, in Paris, where Rilke was attending some anatomy lectures at the École des Beaux-Arts, he made the second of his important connections. "The coronal suture of the skull . . . has . . . a certain similarity to the closely wavy line which the needle of the phonograph engraves on the receiving, rotating cylinder. . . . What if one changed the needle and directed it on its return journey along a tracing which was not derived from the graphic translation of a sound, but existed of itself naturally . . . along the coronal suture, for example." At the present time technicians have done something similar for the movement of the heart, so that death is seen as a straight line, or heard as a continuous drone.

It is of course a fanciful project: to fill the world's cracks with needles that will let us hear those cracks speak. It is only . . . only a poetical idea—a bit inaccurate, too, since it isn't the line but the wiggles in the crevice that matter. The line exists only to allow the vibrations to change, to provide a place for new ones, and to order their appearance in time.

If one can transform the dance of a groove into the sound of a waltz, and if the sound of the waltz can similarly excite the atmosphere so that every ear in the room sympathetically trembles, and if bursts of energy are then sent along many nerves until brain cells light up like Vegas signs and the sound is *heard*—in so many places at once it seems to have filled its space—if all these changes in one chain of cause and effect can take place (go back and forth, actually, like a fan in front of the face), then, Rilke wonders, wouldn't it be possible to translate taste into color, color into sound, sound into the run of an amorous finger along a thigh, for instance: "Is there any contour that one could not, in a sense, complete in this way and then experience it, as it makes itself felt, thus transformed, in another field of sense?"

That is what we have people like Descartes for. A body is reduced to its linear contours. These lines are compactions of dots. Each dot has an address. If the line lies on a plane, two bits of information are required to fix its points; if it lies on a cube or sphere, three pieces are necessary: the location on axes, x-1, y-2, z-3, for instance. Thus any line can be expressed as a set of numbers. Rilke's mind is far away from this sort of transformation, yet his model is not inappropriate. European poetry, he observes, is dominated by the sense of sight (so is its philosophy, as well as its science). "And yet the perfect poem can only materialize on condition that the world, acted upon by all five levers simultaneously, is seen, under a definite aspect, on the supernatural plane, which is, in fact, the plane of the poem."

The poem is like a Persian garden, affecting every sense simultaneously, but it does so by putting itself at a distance advantageous for observation, and placing the various vectors of awareness in the same arena, the area of the poem. The lover, in contrast, because he rushes toward the center of his desires, in closing in—cleaving skin to skin—loses sight of things. We kiss with our eyes closed because there isn't much to see. And if there were, we wouldn't want to see it. Then the rubbing necessary to touch and taste are soon replaced, as the blood rises, by a warmth which overwhelms every other sensation.[1]

By the time he is ready to write "The First Elegy," Rilke has his epistemology worked out.

The material world has scattered about in it, apparently plentifully in some places, less in others, transmitters of various kinds. Signals are constantly being sent by means of air and light out into the surrounding space, where, from time to time, they are picked up by receivers, for there are receivers, too. Our receptivity is determined by the extent and quality of our sensory equipment, by our ability to integrate separate signals into a single coherent experiential "message," and by the width and generosity of attention we are ready to allow ourselves. Pleasure and pain are the result of transmissions, too, as are feelings of joy and fear. Strong and/or threatening communications can narrow our focus to a single source. Persistent interests will cause us to scan the world for certain things rather than others. A person's character can be frequently read through its habitual choice of signal to search for, its openness to experience, and its use of what it receives.

Not only do we miss things because our receivers are limited in number and quality and narrow in focus, but we use sensory cues to tell us what we have in our consciousness; we typecast those clues immediately, conceptualize them, interpret them, and respond, not to experience, which we allow to disappear, but to concepts, to ideas and theories—easier to hold on to and generally furnished with predetermined evaluations and automatic responses. Both Schopenhauer and Bergson were particularly mistrustful of concepts. For Schopenhauer, the replacement of experience by accounts of it created a "corrupt consciousness." For Bergson, concepts falsified experience by dividing its continuities up into discrete blocks the way a motion-picture camera cuts action into a set of stills.

These fears are legitimate, but only if we make a prior mistake, common enough, and certainly critical. Not all properties of the conceptual systems we use to describe experience are characteristics of experience itself. Obviously we can use the German language to talk about the world, to say *Die Welt ist alles was der Fall ist*, or employ arithmetic to measure a room, or use a thermometer to take the temperature of the roast. But

Nature does not speak German, the space of the room is not infinite just because between any of the numbers used to measure it there are an infinite amount more, and 20°C is not twice as hot as 10°C to the leg of lamb. Logical connections do not exist in Nature, only in Logic. And poetry is merely . . . merely poetry.

Duchamps may have moved the urinal out of the john and onto the floor of the museum, calling it a *Fountain*, but that act of defamiliarization will not cause the concept to flee my mind. Quite the contrary. Nevertheless, I can mentally peel off the label (it's a urinal, that's a bicycle wheel atop the kitchen stool, the spiky thing over there is a bottle rack) and contemplate the *Fountain* as a sculptural object. If its basin were awash in piss, detachment would be more difficult. With a cigarette butt afloat there, more difficult still. Yet possible. Then, in that detached and formal state, I can decide whether the *Fountain* merits esthetic appreciation. Duchamps, of course, had another agenda, and was making a different point. He was advancing the projective or label theory of art—with what sincerity it is impossible to know. "If I say it's art, it's art." "If it's in a museum, it's art." Found art, or Ready-Mades, as Duchamps called his, are at best only interesting, or they have local shapes and patches of real quality which you must focus on, ignoring the rest. Occasionally, however, a bit of rusted metal or a once-working tool will allow neglect to turn it into art. As photographs attest, the *Fountain* was more menacing than pleasing. Contemporary urinals have far more style and grace: those, that is, whose enamel, like a white ball gown, flows to the floor.

Animals, Rilke felt, unencumbered by concepts, could look openly out at the world and were more at ease—at one with it—than man. This is Nietzschean. This is romance. Animals are even more "interested" than we are, alert to food signs and danger signals. Rats remember. Squirrels learn. Raccoons adjust. A herd can grow uneasy at the stir of a leaf, a pride become accustomed to human presence, a flock of geese turn aggressive. However, only we have the potentiality for that detachment from the self that yields the purer eye.

Rilke was prepared to push his transformative metaphors quite charmingly far, as he does in a letter of July 15, 1924, to the princesses Mary and Antoinette Windischgraetz:

> In the great cathedrals, in Notre Dame in Paris, St. Mark's, or on Mont St. Michel, I often brought myself to believe that over the centuries the ever-swelling waves of organ music have had some influence on the curves of the arches, the intertwining of the ornaments, or the more customary smoothness of the pillar fluting and of the columns. . . . Do not iron filings form figures when a string is bowed near them?[2]

Rilke makes breathing itself, apart from its olfactory duties, another of our sensory organs. The air we inhale—night air particularly—is the materiality of space itself, which we alter, then, into the space that shall serve our inner world. Moreover, the spoken poem is made of nothing but the poet's breath.

> Breath, you invisible poem!
> The continuous pure exchange
> of our existence with the world's space.
> Counterweight to the rhythm in which I am.
>
> Single wave
> through the slowly forming sea of me;
> among seas the most frugal of all,
> conserving such space.

How many of these waves have been
In me already. Some winds
seem my son.

Do you know me now, breeze, made of my breath?
You, who once were the smooth bark
and foliage round my words.[3]

Although this was the last of the sonnets to arrive, Rilke decided to let it lead off the second part. He then placed another "breath" poem at the conclusion of the entire series.

Silent friend of many distances, feel
how your breath still enlarges space.
From the dark tower let your bell peal.
Whatever feeds upon your face

grows strong from this offering.
Transform matter into mind.
What is the source of your deepest suffering?
If drinking is bitter, become wine.

In this limitless night, be the magical force
at the intersection of your senses,
the meaning of their intercourse.

And if what's earthly no longer knows you,
say to the unmoving earth: I flow.
To the rushing water speak: I stay.[4]

We have already heard Rilke tell lovers to throw the emptiness out of their arms to broaden the spaces we breathe, but now we know that our own breath broadens it. Likewise, in "The First Elegy," the poet's face becomes a pasture. "Oh, then there's Night, when a wind, made from the space where the world resides, feeds on our faces."

To breathe, to see, feel, touch, taste, hear, smell, realize the world, widely, without judgment or repudiation: this was the first task—to allow the world in. To inhale all, to swallow all, to become the place observed. For no more reason than its recognition. Such openness permits the initial transformation that the *Elegies* demand; for when we breathe, when we see, feel, touch, taste, hear the world, we alter its materiality profoundly. What was simply an emitted signal, the outcry of a thing to let us know it was there, becomes a quality in consciousness. The object is visible because its messages can be received, but the message itself is invisible; it is nowhere; or, rather, it is now in an inner space, not the space between our ears, but the space between what our ears hear. Rilke called it "innerworldspace." He liked to imagine that the material world of flux was, with its signaling, beseeching us to become conscious of it, to realize it fully, free it from its grave.

> You earthly things—is this not what you want,
> to arise invisible in us? Is not your dream
> to be one day invisible? Earth!—things!—invisible!
> What, if not this deep translation, is your ardent aim?[5]

Yet Rilke was Mr. Fastidious himself, and that squeamishness, Rilke knew, had to be overcome if he was at last to learn "to see." Contemplation was possible for him—but it was more likely to occur in front of a Cézanne. Most of the revolutionary "new" poems, supposed to demonstrate this saintly openness to objects, are about animals in zoos and flower beds in parks, photographs in books, works of art in the shelter of their museums, figures in myth, icons of the church.

Here we encounter more romance. Animals and birds make noises in order to communicate with one another, flowers use their scent to attract pollinating moths and bees. But many of the signals they send are inadvertent. However stealthily the lion slinks through the tall grass, the grass will sway a little, whisper of the predator's presence. Light falls on unconcerned surfaces and is reflected back to us unsent by any solid, bearing no petition.

As Rilke knew, and knew better than he cared to, normal experience is interested, not contemplative. People don't perceive an IT, they perceive what that IT means. The poet as a person is no exception.

> Yes, the springtimes have needed you. There've been stars
> to solicit your seeing. In the past, perhaps,
> waves rose to greet you, or out an open window,
> as you passed, a violin was giving itself
> to someone. This was a different commandment.
>
> But could you obey it? Weren't you always
> anxiously peering past them, as though
> they announced a sweetheart's coming? (Where would you
> have hidden her, with those heavy foreign thoughts
> tramping in and out and often staying overnight?)[6]

When we perceive fully, and do the work assigned to us, the world becomes glorious. Then "it is breathtaking just to be here."

However, I feel obliged to say, when we perceive fully, we do ourselves a favor, not the world.

I doubt if Rilke ever read a word of Immanuel Kant's, but when two "great minds" are right about something, why shouldn't they seem to say the same thing? The esthetic experience is not mediated by concepts. It displays disinterested interest, and appreciates purposiveness independently of any purpose.

Rilke does not understand how the transformation of matter into mind works, but we should not blame him for that. No one does. After several thousand years of wondering, we still don't know. Although materialists will be happy to explain to us how the nervous system functions, and hope we shall confuse this explanation, as marvelous and detailed as it is, with an account of the character of consciousness and how consciousness came to be, they are not a step closer to crossing that threshold. We may not know how our awareness got here, but Rilke believes he knows what its purpose is: to make the signals we receive from external things into inner, and hence invisible, manifestations—the invisible visibly invisible, if you like.

When we experience things as we at least sometimes should, the psychological distance between them and ourselves disappears. We are what we perceive, and what we perceive exists nowhere but in us. We touch. Neither of us is any longer lonely. It constitutes what E. F. N. Jephcott calls "the privileged moment" in his excellent study *Proust and Rilke: The Literature of Expanded Consciousness.*[7]

We should not imagine that such moments involve the cancellation of the self. A union is not a cancellation. What has to be left out of the self is its selfishness, but not its particular quality of mind. Nor could we afford to prolong such states of awareness or increase their frequency even if we could, because living does demand selection, utility, and action.

Nevertheless, this saintly acceptance of life is an obligation laid upon all of us . . . "a kind of commandment." In Henry

James' version the injunction is: try to be someone on whom nothing is lost. James, however, is asking us to be quick, clever, and deep about interpreting social signals; he is advising us not to enjoy the look of haystacks in the rain, but to catch signs of adultery in an eyelid, doubt in a pause. From the Austen/James/Wharton point of view, Rilke lived little in society; he just visited it from time to time.

Rilke's inwarding does have a level of "interpretation," however, though it probably wouldn't satisfy James. If the world awaits realization by an accomplished human mind, then the world should have wants and wishes, which would mean it, too, has an interior, so that the expressions on the faces of things might allow us to read the state of their inwardness, *as if* they too were alive. We habitually infer the contents of another's innerworldspace from his or her outerworldactions. In a Sherlock Holmesian mood we may also read anger or impatience in the forcibly stubbed cigarette butt, haste in a spill of gravel, weariness in signs of wear and tear, meanness in the root that trips us up, loneliness in the atmosphere of a rented room, willfulness in a twitch or tic. *The Notebooks of Malte Laurids Brigge* has much animism of this kind throughout its early pages.

Furthermore, the use which clothes receive—and books suffer, and pots and pans undergo, and windowsills and stoops endure—this use wears and soils and pits them, mars and creases and scars them, so that gradually, and over time, these effects will shape a surface that resembles their life, reflecting there all that history has done to them, everything they've labored to achieve. Rust destroys, but it creates character more surely than most playwrights. Aging delights in lines.

To observe the brook gurgling happily, to enter a gloomy wood with trepidation, to feel the melancholy of a motel room, to appreciate the sturdy character of a scar-faced loading-dock door, to shudder some in front of a broken window, does not mean one has returned to a state of mana worship, or even that one has simply made an emotional mistake, for a mountain can seem menacing even to a positivist who not only knows better, but bets both top and bottom dollar on it. For Rilke the world has an expressive surface, and its "look" should not be ignored when we look.

If the first transformation is everyone's obligation, the second transformation is more pointedly a task for the poet. The language of ordinary use suffers the same fate as those of functional things—silverware, tea service, pin-striped suits. Paul Valéry's distinction between dancing and walking (not strolling) is after the same game. Customarily, we look past the word to its referent, or into the word for its idea. If we reach the referent, we again look beyond, this time at its importance to us; and when we dig out the idea, we take it, like a nugget, to be assayed. Normally, we do not listen to the music the syllables sing; we don't appreciate the conceptual connections a word has made in its life; we don't understand why Adam was asked to "name" the animals—for we don't know that naming is knowing. According to the *Elegies*, we are here just to utter. To sew concept to referent like a button on a coat . . . a button meant not to button but to be.

You might think we were on the stage, we've been asked to make so many changes. Well, of course, we are, and in "The Fifth Elegy" we shall watch our own heart's curtain rise. (Change 1): our self must become selfless, in order (Change 2) fully and unreservedly to accept the world, making matter into consciousness, and following these (Change 3) to alter the medium of what will be an artwork so that it is ready to serve a purposeless purpose. Think, as Thales did, of stream and steam, lava and ice: one substance having many modes of life. Believe, as Heraclitus did, in the perpetual flux, in unceasing metamorphosis, in the caterpillar's pupal sleep, its nymphhood, and its butterflying form.

Will transformation. Be inspired by the flame
where a thing made of Change conceals itself;
this informing spirit, master of all that's earthly,
loves nothing more than the moment of turning.
What's heartset on survival is already stony;
how safe is it, hid in its innocuous gray?
Look out, from afar a far harder hardness warns it:
feel the approach of a hammer held high.

Whoever flows forth from himself like a freshet, Knowledge
    will acknowledge,
and lead him, entranced, through her wondrous world,
where endings are often beginnings and beginnings ends.

Every fortune-favored space you wander through, astonished,
is the child or the grandchild of Change. Even Daphne,
as she leafs into laurel, wants to feel you become wind.[8]

Language restored to its purity is ready to praise. The fourth metamorphosis requires the poet to make a verbal object from the previous transformations, and insert it into the world. Such an object will, in a sense, be material again, public, no longer invisible. Its reason for existing will be its own inherent value. Mont Sainte-Victoire will have passed through the painter's gaze into immateriality only to return through his art to the canvas. It is no longer a mountain. It is a mountain seen. Seen superbly. Seen from Les Lauves, seen from Bibemus Quarry. Seen not by Cézanne the man but (to adopt the formula of Gertrude Stein) by the human mind. It will, however, be more than a mountain so supremely seen, because it will have been transmogrified by the painter's paints, the painter's artistry, the art itself. Now it will no longer need to resemble. If the easel has to be brought to the mountain, the mountain must move toward the easel. In the case of the poet, the perception will have soaked for a long time in a marinade of mind, in a slather of language, in a history of poetic practice. The resulting object will not be like other objects; it will have been invested with consciousness, the consciousness of the artist. Then we, as we read, see, hear, shall share this other superior awareness. We shall be Bach, be Keats, be Cézanne, again, not as they were as men—who desires that?—but as they are as artists.

And when Auden watches Icarus fall and completes his poem about it, we shall be able to read the poet weighing Breughel as he weighs the world. It is a perception which paintings have let the poet have. And so the indebtedness proceeds, threatening regressions in both directions. Let them be. They are benign.

BLUE HYDRANGEA

Like the green that cakes in a pot of paint,
these leaves are dry, dull and rough
behind this billow of blooms whose blue
is not their own but reflected from far away
in a mirror dimmed by tears and vague,
as if it wished them to disappear again
the way, in old blue writing paper,
yellow shows, then violet and gray;

a washed-out color as in children's clothes
which, no longer worn, no more can happen to:
how much it makes you feel a small life's brevity.

But suddenly the blue shines quite renewed
within one cluster, and we can see
a touching blue rejoice before the green.[9]

This sonnet is made of many observations, some information, one metaphor for the leaves, three more for the petals, and one conclusion in the first triplet. When we translate *Hortensia*, which is the name these flowers have in Europe (so called after the mistress of a French botanist), we lose one meaning and gain another (which the "water cup" shape of the seedpods supplies). This plant is like litmus paper. In alkaline soils the blooms are likely to be pink; under acid conditions they are likely to be blue. Aluminum sulfate will provoke the plant in the blue direction; lime will intensify the pink. My grandmother buried nails near her hydrangea, and they bloomed blue as jeans.

The petals do fade toward a dirty beige, with a little yellow appearing, a bit of purple, too, as the poem says. Here we have a rather namby-pamby soil, and this is what the distant mirror reflects. The color is "washed-out." The blue shade of old writing paper also pales in a similar way. The poem proceeds through three fades: a teary mirror, a faded letter, worn-out children's clothes. The brevity of a small life: petal, paper, child—and all they stand for. Until a spot more fertile for the flower is found, and the blue is suddenly renewed, whereupon it rejoices as one risen might. This, then, is a poem of consolation.

Little more than a year later, Rilke writes another *Hortensia* poem. This plant bears pink blossoms, perhaps because it is not a sonnet, but the roles of the petals and the leaves are reversed. The flowers are giving away their scent, hoping perhaps, with this generosity, to escape a decolorization. However, the poet observes that underneath the pink of the petals, the plant's leaves have grasped the situation. Their green is going, as though they wanted to be a reminder of what must come, because the leaves understand the inevitable. No consolation here, only a memento mori.

Do we need to be told? No. These are simply . . . simply poems. It is the quality of the awareness encapsulated here that counts. The teardrop in a distant mirror which speaks to us of vanity perhaps or beauty's loss; the billet-doux whose ink has probably faded, too; the folded children's clothes about to be buried in an attic hamper: advancing stages of life that are most delicately invoked, so sadly sensed, little losses everywhere to brighten by contrast one sudden blue renewal. The poem's final line, then, is both positive and pathetic.

The poem transforms many things—precepts, facts, feelings, memories, rhythms, words—and represents them. It is now a verbal "thing"—an object unlike the leaves, which are said "to know" but really know nothing; an object which is a complex bit of human awareness of the world, an awareness of which we become aware ourselves . . . and then again . . . and then again . . .

Many grow impatient with what, in Rilke, they see as an escapist view of art: this emphasis on Being rather than on Doing, on relinquishment rather than retention, on acceptance rather than revision; it smacks more of moral indolence than saintliness to them; and its radical subjectivity is offensively antisocial and indifferent to the collective.

The desire to improve the world, and therefore the condition of the people who occupy and who despoil it, is, however compassionate, an impulse born of ignorance and arrogance.

To wish to better a person's situation presupposes a degree of insight into his circumstances that even a writer does not enjoy regarding a character born of his own imagina-

tion. . . . To wish to change, to better a person's situation
means to give him, in exchange for difficulties in which he
is practiced and experienced, other difficulties which may
find him even more helpless.[10]

Here is another example of how cleverly Rilke hid behind the
truth (or a partial truth) and concealed his unconcern.

Yet the *Elegies*, over and over, denounce the times, most particularly their cheap pleasures and their commercial culture.

> Squares, O square in Paris, ceaseless showplace,
> where the *modiste* Madame Lamort
> weaves and winds the restless ways of the world,
> those endless ribbons, into ever new designs:
> bows, frills, flowers, cockades, artificial fruit,
> each cheaply dyed, to decorate
> the tacky winter hats of Fate.[11]

Surely, in these sentiments, Rilke is not out of line. "The Tenth
Elegy" is particularly fierce.

> Oh, how completely would an Angel crush underfoot their
>   market of cheap comforts,
> with the church at its side, purchased ready-made,
> as swept, as shut, as disappointing as a post office on a
>   Sunday. . . .

> Especially worth seeing, but for adults only: coins in
>   copulation,
> right there on stage, money's metal genitals
>   rubadubdubbing.
> Educational, and sure to stimulate multiplication . . .

Denounce is all he does. Rilke has no program for social reform. Our problems are basically metaphysical and cannot be voted out of office or, their heads on pikes, paraded through the streets. Again reflecting Rilke's stoicism, the human condition (as it has come to be called) can only be understood, appreciated, and endured.

> We're not in tune. Not like migratory birds.
> Outmoded, late, in haste, we force ourselves on winds
> which let us down upon indifferent ponds.[12]

We are not at one with Nature the way the animals are. Actually, we surround ourselves with ourselves (farms, towns, cities, nations, education, technology, art) to blot Nature out, only to find no soul is reachable, touchable, knowable, but our own. And it? Left begging to belong. Rilke suffered, as Nietzsche did, and many others before him, from an envy of the animal. The grace of the big cat, the eagle's easy soaring, the spider's patience—qualities we so desperately desire—are granted to these creatures along with their furs and feathers as a birthright. And the bees hive, starlings flock, cows herd, geese fly together north to south, reading the air, knowing towns and times. Alas for us, as Plotinus wrote: life is the flight of the alone to the alone.

This is not the worst of the *Elegies'* mistakes, though it is half-baked ideas of this kind which lead many people to dismiss poetry as merely poetry. They know that instinct—the source of blind repetition—is a species of stupidity. Instinct opposes change; it cannot cope with difference.

Nor does one need another ideology to reject Rilke's view that life and death are in the same continuum as though one were infrared and the other ultraviolet. Plato, in the *Phaedo*, strug-

gling with the idea of significant contraries and the problem of
relations, tries to argue for the immortality of the soul by suggesting that life is dependent upon death the way warmth is
connected to cold; that the life/death continuum is therefore a
matter of degree; and that without death (as is the case with
"right" and "left" and "high" and "low") we could not understand
or possess life. One is made from or comes out of the other: the
cold can be said to "cause" warmth, and short things make tall
ones possible. Rilke makes this point repeatedly. But the argument first confuses a condition like death (which is not a matter
of degree) with dying (which is). If I am not running but standing still, my stationary condition should not be understood as
very slow running, or my running, when it occurs, as very fast
standing. The argument also assumes that if two terms must be
defined jointly, because our *understanding* of one requires our
understanding of the other, then the *existence* of these states or
qualities is equally interdependent. We cannot infer from the
fact that good and evil are correlative terms (if it is a fact) that
Paradise, in order to be Paradise, must have its snake. The most
we can conclude is that if there were a perfect place, the people
there would be unaware of its perfection, just as the good book
says. Adam and Eve know neither good nor evil until they've
eaten of the apple.

> Plump apple, banana, gooseberry, pear,
> speak life and death into the mouth.
> I have seen them there. I swear . . .
> on a child's face when eating them.
> This comes from far . . . from far.
> What's slowly growing nameless in your mouth?
> Freed from the fruit's flesh,
> where words once were, the juices of discovery are.

How can you call this "apple."
This sweetness that feels at first so dense
and reluctant, yielding slowly to the tongue,

until it clarifies, becomes awake, transparent,
doubly meant, sunny, earthy, wholly here:
Oh, such touching, carnal knowing, joy—immense.[13]

Dying is indeed a diminished form of life, but there is no realm of the dead where the dead dwell like shades cast into an underworld. It may be possible to die your own death, as Rilke also believed, by making your death a clear consequence of your "way" of living, and in that sense growing your death inside you. Moreover, one could refuse the ministrations of doctors and the help of hospitals—dying on your own—alone. Howling, as the Chamberlain's death howls in *The Notebooks of Malte Laurids Brigge*.

The seed image serves Rilke well. As the tree reaches fruition, and realizes the purpose of its growing; as flowers flower and exemplify theirs; as couples couple, too, to produce anew; so pods and fruit appear, only to fall and rot or lose their life between a child's greedy jaws, or, shaken by a breeze, to reseed the earth for another season, populate a meadow with Queen Anne's lace and goldenrod. Life thus passes from one body to another, and we all must make way for the vast numbers who are coming; yet it is not my life, nor yours, that seeds itself in a son or daughter, to rise again and look out with refreshed eyes, no, it is just life as life—life that has no single owner.

Thomas Hardy, who is also a very great poet, tackles this kind of transmigration, as he always tackles his topics, head on, in some lines written after Louisa Harding, whom he'd been sweet on as a boy, died well along, at seventy-two.

Portion of this yew
Is a man my grandsire knew,
Bosomed here at its foot:
This branch may be his wife,
A ruddy human life
Now turned to a green shoot.

These grasses must be made
Of her who often prayed,
Last century, for repose;
And the fair girl long ago
Whom I often tried to know
May be entering this rose.

So, they are not underground,
But as nerves and veins abound
In the growths of upper air,
And they feel the sun and rain,
And the energy again
That made them what they were![14]

Like so many of the sentiments expressed in the *Elegies*, these thoughts are more than a bit balderdashy. In this poem, nothing asserted or surmised can possibly be so. Yet the sentiment expressed is everywhere splendid. Nor may we imagine, even for a moment, that Hardy believes that a portion of this yew is a man his grandsire knew. So what does he believe? Will he pick the rose his fair girl may have entered, mow the grass? How is one to reconcile the facts (false) and the sentiments (goody, they are not underground, what a comfort!) with what I take to be the excellence of the poem—a poem whose sole purpose, it appears, is to make the poet momentarily feel better?

Can the poet really wish his fair girl were entering a rose? What is genuine here, beyond the rhyme? Is poetry the elevation of silliness into the sublime? Speaking of the silly sublime, let us risk blindness and take a look at the Angels.

Why are the Angels of the *Elegies* so fortunate, so superior, in the poet's eye? Each one is sufficient unto itself. Everything that streams out of them returns like an echo. They pass through the realms of life and death without feeling a tweak of difference. If we joined Leibniz to Berkeley for a moment, we might imagine the Angels as monads possessed of a deity's power to perceive. God first anticipates our existence (we plan a picnic), then He directly makes us exist (we have our picnic), then afterward he remembers the way we were (we recall the picnic). We could say, then, that we'd always been, and would always be, so long as God, our Author, continued to plan for and expect us, steadily perceive us, and faithfully remember. A novel does no less.

Everything that's mirrored in a monad's mind would exist on that single plane—as one kind of perception or other—and a whole history could unroll like a tapestry or the carvings on a triumphant pillar, or simply be read—anticipated and remembered—like the words of a text. Countries which fear foreign influences like to become "self-sufficient," as the hermit does, the sage who sits in front of his mountain cave slowly ruminating on his gnomic wisdom; but individual self-sufficiency, obviously desirable up to a point, becomes dangerously antisocial in ways that are quite obvious. Rilke's Angels, that is, have little to recommend them as ideal states for human beings. However, they are models of perfection which a formalist esthetic might advance as admirable for works of art.

A work of art, from this point of view, is complete and self-contained. That does not mean that it makes no reference to the world. Monads are worlds in themselves. It does not mean that the work cannot depend upon information that must be found elsewhere. The explanation of every word in a poem lies elsewhere: the nature of hydrangeas, for instance. The poem does not require every quality these plants possess, but it calls on some, and pulls them into its orbit. The poem practices close observation, but the accuracy it displays is necessary only because otherwise it would draw the wrong information from the reader. Called "Blue Asters," it would fail the litmus test. If the flowers are fictional, as characters in a novel are, the exactitude of observation (number, closeness, aptness of details, for instance) need only be mimicked; its precision can be as fictional as the rest; however, here, the point of the poem is that the flowers are not fictional, but appear and reappear in our lives like lacy Victorian valentines—maybe quaint, but prized.

Formal perfection is equivalent to internal justification. If someone cries "Fire!" in a crowded theater, there'd better be a fire; if someone cries "Fire!" and the firing squad does, there will be an order to appeal to to justify the killing, not so easily a reason to find; and if someone recites

> This ae nighte, this ae nighte,
> Every nighte and alle,
> Fire and fleet and candle-lighte,
> And Christe receive thy saule

then a belief in God, God's Son, in sin, in having sinned, and consequently the need and yearning for salvation may explain the occurrence of the prayer, but the formal order of the dirge will suffice for its nature. Then I may sing these lines, in Benjamin Britten's harrowing setting of them, any time I wish, even though a pagan, unneedy and unshriven. And their feeling will be never more genuine or "meant" or necessary.

When the animals emerge from the forest to hear Orpheus

sing, they form a magic circle and suffer a sea change. They enter a peaceable kingdom very unlike the war-filled world they just left. If I bring a revolver onstage during a play, or, like Beckett's Winnie, I pull it out of my bag, even though it may be as real as the murder it might occasion in ordinary life, it is now a prop and can make only prop noise when it goes off, cause a fake bullet to fly, inflict only a simulated wound and, in pretended consequence, an actor's feigned collapse into a role-real death, followed by a life-real rise at the curtain's fall. The space of the poem is similarly transformative.

Words are not just changed there, they are made. For what in the world does "fleet" mean? Well, there is a "brig" in the second stanza.

> From Brig o' Dread when thou may'st pass,
> Every nighte and alle,
> To Purgatory fire thou com'st at last;
> And Christe receive thy saule.

How does it help, this brig? I think: not at all. Some have suggested "sleet" should take its place, or "salt." Salt? If I were forced to make a substitution, it would be "flight." Fortunately, I don't have to. Confounded curiosity leads me to look the word up: its etymology is probably "float" or "swim." So I am swimming past the brig o' dread on my way to hell, when . . . ? Leave "fleet" alone. I know "fleet" no better than "wabe," yet in time, and after repeated recitations, I happily gyre and gimbel in the wabe, and I fear fire, fleet, and candle-lighte, and am stricken with awe—though I perhaps perversely think this word I don't know the meaning of should be spelled "flete." Still, playing dumb won't clinch the argument. As with "wabe," I know what "fleet" means in this context. "Everything fleeting concerns us, we most fleeting of all." "Fleet" means more than "fleeting," however—a whole lot more. "Fire and fleet and candle-lighte" are a wondrous trio—creating one another as they go.

Such space is Angel space, such life is Angel life, where everything is experienced like daydream theater, self-enclosed and without consequence. Daydreams can have consequences, of course. Some of them are rehearsals for a seduction (say) which might actually take place. Plays make money or fold. Consequences? Not when one is imagining that some wooden **O** holds the vasty fields of France.

Attempts to break out of the frame, extend the apron of the stage, push into the audience (plant actors in it, enlist it, attack it), or use illusion or other ruses to heighten verismo, to journalize: each demonstrates the power of the art's domain. It becomes as elastic as a rubber face, little dotted lines rush out and around every extension, and the audience isn't insulted or actually frightened, the planted actors didn't pay their way, nor do Céline's raging pages hurt our hands. The reader is in the magic circle, too. There he may entertain the most sublime, the most harrowing, the most merry, the most morose, of ideas as if he were serving tea to friends.

> Who makes the death of a child out of gray bread,
> or leaves it there to harden in the round mouth
> like the ragged core of a sweet apple?[15]

The shock of these lines is mock shock. Admiration is genuine. "Out of gray bread," "to harden in the round mouth" "the ragged core of a sweet apple." Words like these set the mind free of the world. Free to see and feel afresh the very world it's been freed from.

However, as I've previously indicated, Rilke didn't want the *Elegies* to be self-contained *Dinge* like the *New Poems*. He had begun his career as a poet of effusion, then trained himself to be a poet of reception; now (it is 1914, the same year as "The Great Night") he needed to become a poet of internal intensity. Before he could pour forth again, he would have to work on himself and all the material he had stored like compost for a garden. I have already quoted a few lines from the poem that expresses this necessity as he saw it, and his forlornness and blind self-absorption in front of a war he was probably unaware was coming. The poem demonstrates, as his laments so often did, that Rilke had really nothing to complain about. He was actually at the height of his Orphic power.

TURNING-POINT

The way from an intense inwardness to greatness passes through sacrifice.
                                        For Rudolf Kassner

For a long time his gaze had achieved it.
Stars would be brought to their knees
by the force of his upflung vision,
or he would kneel himself to scrutinize,
and the fragrance from this insistence
would drowsy a god,
till it slept in the smile that it smiled at him.

Towers he would stare at so
they were startled from their shapes—
restoring them suddenly in a storm of stones!
But how often the landscape,

worn down by daylight,
came to rest in his quiet perceiving, at evening.

Animals entered his open look
like a meadow, trustingly grazed there;
even the imprisoned lions
peered in, as though on a strange species of freedom;
birds flew straight and easy through a space
which felt their flight;
flowers gazed back at him
as large as they are for children.

And the rumor that a Seer was about
stirred the dimly,
more dubiously visible—
stirred the women.
How long had this looking lasted?
How long had his soul fasted?
gone begging in the depths of his glance?

When he, whose profession was Waiting, stayed in strange
        towns, the hotel's
bemused and preoccupied bedroom
morosely contained him, and in the avoided mirror
the room presided again,
and, later, in the tormenting bed,
yet again—
where this adjudicating air,
in a manner beyond understanding,
passed judgment upon his heart—whose beating could
        barely be felt
through its painful burial in his body—

and pronounced this hardly felt heart
to be lacking in love.

(And denied him any further devotions.)

For such looking, you see, has its limits.
And your simply gazed-over world
wants to grow greater through love.

The work of the eye is complete now;
work next at the heart's work—
on those images you've captured within you,
led in and overcome and left unknown.
Look—inside bridegroom—on your inside bride,
so superbly drawn out of a thousand natures:
a beauty thus far won,
but thus far never loved.[16]

If the persona of the poet plainly presides in most of these
lyrics of lamentation and self-scrutiny (as one might expect),
while a universalized "I" is the speaker of the *Elegies*, most of
the *Dingegedicht* ("The Panther," "Torso of an Archaic Apollo,"
"Blue Hydrangea," and "Death"), as well as many of the *Sonnets to Orpheus*, emerge from a voice not unlike that of a
moral and esthetic conscience: either directly, "You must
change your life," or indirectly, as if the poet were saying,
"And you should have seen, felt, thought this, too." Does eating an apple (even in special circumstances) give us immense
joy? No. But perhaps it ought to. In a machine-made world,
in a world of multiplying masses and increasing commer-
cialism, where heads by the millions are filled with vulgar
images, stupid thoughts, and crass pleasures, it is incumbent
on those of us who wish to "rise above ourselves" (and hence

above others) to perform first the hard holy work of the eye and then the painful hidden work of the heart. We are not here to praise the Lord, but to praise the world, to show the Angel—*things*.

Praise this world to the Angel, not the unutterable one.
You cannot impress *him* with the splendor you've felt,
for in the heaven of heavens, where he feels so sublimely,
you're but a beginner. Show him some simple thing, then,
that's been changed in its passage through human ages
till it lives in our hands, in the shine of our eyes, as a part
of ourselves. Tell him *things*. He'll stand more astonished,
as you stood by the roper in Rome or the potter in Egypt.
Show him how happy a thing can be, how innocent and ours;
how even Sorrow, in the midst of lamenting, is determined
    to alter,
to serve as a thing, or fade in a thing—to escape
into beauty beyond violining. These things whose life
is a constant leaving, they know when you praise them.
Transient, they trust us, the most transient, to come
to their rescue; they wish us to alter them utterly,
within our invisible hearts, into—so endlessly—us!
Whoever we may finally be.[17]

By now, Rilke's psychological patterns should be fairly clear. First, he expects of ordinary life far more than it can possibly produce in any regular way. Second, he consequently enters a state of dismay and disappointment. Third, he requires of the poet that he lead an elevated life anyway. Fourth, the poet, in order to lead that elevated life, is forced to accept and praise the same ordinary world he began by disdaining.

In short, an absolute intimacy is demanded. Then, when this is found to be impossible, the effort to love is redoubled. Love that's unrequited, love without any physical involvement, love which will last because it is almost a private unseen state of the soul, becomes the higher obligation. Everything is in flux, therefore we should embrace change. Why?—in order to remain. "Who speaks of victory? To endure is everything."

And if what's earthly no longer knows you,
say to the unmoving earth: I flow.
To the rushing water speak: I stay.[18]

The death of a young woman, before her life has really begun, is awful, therefore we shall celebrate it; childhood is misery, so we shall call it wonderful, innocent and open. Heritage is status, so we shall deny our Czech past, refuse to be labeled a German, find that everything Austrian disgusts us, regret that our parents live on like monsters inside us, and, because we believe each man is a multitude—of ogres and urges going back to the primeval slime—we shall require, in its stead, to see Unity . . . Oneness: Maninkindness, if I may sound German. Using our carefully created higher awareness, we should seek the simple openness of the animal. Aloof from the mob, we nevertheless join it—to cancel the count. Hoping to merge with all things, celebrate distance. Practice makes perfect, but as "The Fifth Elegy" warns, perfection soon shows itself to be empty and sterile. And if we observe our own heart's curtain lift to display a thoroughly bourgeois performance (as we do in the fourth), shall we boo and catcall?

Hey! I'm waiting. Even if the lights go out;
even if I'm told, "That's all"; even if absence
drifts toward me like a gray draft from the stage;
even if none of my ancestors will sit silently by me anymore,

nor a woman, nor the boy with the squinting brown eyes:
I'll stay in my seat. One can always watch.

Over and over again, Rilke takes away with one hand, and
gives with another. What he takes away may have been a gift,
but what he gives is always a task. Life is not a song, he says, so
sing!

In sum: we live only once, and everything that fills this life,
we shall have only once—once and no more. And what is this
life but our awareness of ourselves and our awareness of the
world? Alas, most of this consciousness of ours is narrowed,
perverted, and wasted by the burdens of daily life. We can try
to save ourselves through love, which turns out only too often
to be an attempt to possess someone or something, to hold
back the flux (love me forever!), but also to obstruct the loved
one's freedom. If the world awaits our seeing, if our duty is
to give consciousness to things, that consciousness will disappear with bitter quickness, for we are the most fragile of all. So
what is to be done? Leave that consciousness behind as a quality of our created things; deposit it in the forms and textures we
give to objects. But our created things are mostly crushed and
tossed away after use like daily newspapers or concert programs. We care only for power, and, having it, do what? Go to
war for more, consume the fruits of the earth, make paper
cups from which to drink our *Todlos*, "the dark bitter beer so
sweet to the addicted, so long as they swallow it while chewing
on fresh distractions." Those few attainments which display the
grace of great things, we must take into ourselves and save from
an indifferent multitude. Because all our knowledge, even the
gift of a pleasant life, comes to nothing if we know more, enjoy
more, only to destroy more. "The Seventh Elegy" comes right
out with it.

My love, the world exists nowhere but within us.
Withinwarding is everything. The outer world
dwindles, and day fades from day. Where once
a solid house was, soon some invented structure
perversely suggests itself, as at ease among ideas
as if it still stood in the brain.
The Present has amassed vast stores of power,
shapeless as the vibrant energy it has stolen from the earth.
It has forgotten temples. We must save in secret
such lavish expenditures of spirit.
Yes, even where one thing we served, knelt for, and
prayed to survives, it seeks to see itself invisible.
Many have ceased perceiving it, and so will miss
the chance to enlarge it, add pillars and statues, give it
grandeur, within.

These lines could be, and have been, understood as solipsistic, but that is a misreading. Rilke realizes the material world exists apart from him (and indifferently), and he knows that there are other modes of awareness, but it remains true that, for each of us, our consciousness is our only proof we live—we live in it—it is all we are. About this, I believe, Rilke was right. "Doing" that is not "improving" is pointless, and "improving" is illusory if it is not an end in itself.

The reader must retain a head clear enough to realize that Rilke's inwarding of life depends entirely upon a detachment from it. It is not "living" life he asks for but its contemplation. "Living" paradoxically requires ignoring things, forgetting things, enshrining partiality, obeying interest, changing your situation, not simply observing it change; living is wanting; living is willful, heedless, fearful; living absorbs life; living feeds; living excretes; living is as brutal and indifferent as chewing teeth.

There is a much-quoted passage from a letter Rilke wrote during the early days of the First World War to the Princess Marie von Thurn und Taxis-Hohenlohe which I feel obliged to quote again. In a world in which Mammon and Moloch are the real gods worshiped, where are we to find consolation? Ironically, in the inherent capacities of mankind.

It is certain that the divinest consolation is contained in humanity itself—we would not be able to do much with the consolations of a god; only that our eye would have to be a trace more seeing, our ear more receptive, the taste of a fruit would have to penetrate us more completely, we would have to endure more odor, and in touching and being touched be more aware and less forgetful—: in order promptly to absorb out of our immediate experiences consolations that would be more convincing, more preponderant, more true than all the suffering that can ever shake us to our very depths.[19]

"The Seventh Elegy" wonders whether we have anything to show the Angels, anything which will justify our existence, or is it all rape, plunder, murder, and thoughtless, pointless consumption? If we are all alone here, if we are going nowhere else but underground, if we shall never even enter a rose again, then what have we done? *what have we done!* to justify the life of man—our sojourn, our abiding here—for it's not been our service that offers itself for accounting, but our wasted opportunities, our suicides . . .

> There stands Death, a blue residue
> in a cup without a saucer.

An odd spot for a cup:
balanced on the back of a hand.
One can clearly see along its glazed
curve a crack showing where the handle snapped.
Dusty. And HOPE on its side in washed-out letters.

The one who was to drink this drink
spelled it out at breakfast long ago.

What sort of specters are these, then,
who have to have a poison push them off?

Otherwise would they remain? Would they gnaw on
this food full of hindrance forever?

One must pull the harsh present
from them like a set of false teeth.
Only then they mumble. Mumble . . . umble . . .
umble . . . .

O shooting star,
seen from a bridge once, a penetrating ray:
Never to forget you. Stay.[20]

Never to forget, either . . . our homicides, our patricides and
matricides and fratricides, our infanticides, our genocides, and
our incessant gnaw and natter, our ruin of the world—even to
its outer edges.

But one tower was great, wasn't it? O Angel, it was—
even compared to you? Chartres was great—

and music rose even higher, flew far beyond us.
Even a woman in love, alone at night by her window . . .
didn't she reach your knee?[21]

Congratulations are in order. Reaching an Angel's knee is a stretch.

ERECT NO MEMORIAL STONE

Singing is Being. This is what Rilke knew to the inner marrow of his bones. The paper, the ink, the fingers, moving as in Fitzgerald's sappy Persian poem. Having writ, they move on to other writing. Knowing that his words cannot be canceled. Because, I believe, Rilke felt himself to be a failure and a fraud except when he was writing. Then he was the writer who he wished was the man he wasn't. Then he was the lover he hoped could—as we say now—commit. Rilke understood his shortcomings so thoroughly that his knowing was a shortcoming. But on the page, in a poem, the contradictions which were his chief affliction could be reconciled. There he could answer every question with "I praise."

> Tell us, poet, what do you do?
>   —I praise.
> But the dreadful, the monstrous, and their ways,
> how do you stand them, suffer it all?
>   —I praise.
> But the anonymous, featureless days,
> how, poet, can you ask them to call?
>   —I praise.
> What chance have you, in so many forms,

under each mask, to speak a true phrase?
                      —I praise.
And that the calm as well as the crazed
know you like star and storm?
                    —because I praise.[1]

Those dashes read to me like replacements for "nevertheless." Through gritted teeth. Nor, of course, did this poet always "praise." Tell us, poet, what do you do? —I lament. The word *klage* clangs to mark each passing hour. The poet laments the life he must lead. He laments the women he writes his love letters to, whose friendship he has formed, whose hearts he has forced to harden. He laments the death they bring . . . in a poem whose first stanza also dwindles.

"Man must die because he has known them." Die
of their smile's evanescent bloom. Die
of their delicate hands. Die
of women.

The word comes to his rescue. As it has in the past. As it will again. Even in a world where the word is imperiled. Why is it breathtaking to be here? How, in a life of suffering, does one painless moment redeem the rest? Are all the disappointments and duties of love worth the exuberant feeling of both power and need in lust's overswollen opinion of itself?

Let the young man sing of these bringers of death
while they soar through the space of his heart.
From his swelling breast
let him sing to them:
the unattainable! Ah, how far off they are.

Over the peaks
of his passion they glide and pour
a sweetly transfigured darkness
into the forsaken valley of his arms.
The wake of their rising ruffles the leaves of his body.
His streams run sparkling into the distance.

But the grown man
shivers and is silent. He who,
pathless, has wandered through the night
in the rocky ridges of his feelings:
is silent.

As the sailor is silent, the old-timer,
and the terrors he has endured
rattle around inside him as though in shaken cages.[2]

Shivering and silence. First it is the layers of the young lover's body which women ruffle; then it is the shivering of the mature man, who remembers his confused wanderings; finally it is the old sailor, deep in memory too, his terrors trapped inside him. In the familiar interior landscape of "the mountains of the heart," with its forsaken valleys and last hamlets of feeling, the poet falls silent, because once he has experienced the terrors of love, he will no longer sing of women; they shall not have a letter of his praise.

Orpheus did not fare well at their hands—hands which tore him to pieces. So unless the women are both young and dead, the poet will not praise—he'll blame.

Why is the description of women as death-bringers acceptable here? Is it because women are the bearers of life, and therefore make death possible? Is it because of the little death we are alleged to suffer in sexual transports? Is it because women, domestically inclined, hold men back from their greatest triumphs, tethering them to the earth and to day-to-day existence? Or is it because, in front of them and the lure of their flesh, men are disarmed, confronted with their own infantile yearnings? the poet at the breast? Or is it because, in failing to perform, some men realize a divided attraction? If you mistrust mothers, must you mistrust all the others?

Women are carriers of Christianity. Enslaved by the system, women represent the system. Women, barred from all the business of the world, have learned how to manipulate the men who manipulate it. These thoughts could be from a speech Nietzsche might have made.

Just ahead of the composition, in 1915, of "The Fourth Elegy," Rilke wrote seven so-called phallic poems. Their inadequacies are sufficient to form a parade. The vagina is variously a garden, a grove, a heaven, a soft night into which the poet will fire his "womb-dazzling rocket," and it is a tomb, too, in which his cock, now a stiff corpse, will be buried. Of course it will rise again, this stiff corpse, but it will be death rising, death alive at last, to die once more. "Already your unwitting command raises the column in my genital-woodsite," John Mood was apparently not embarrassed to write when he translated these really wretched pieces for his collection *Rilke on Love and Other Difficulties*.[3] The penis is a tree, a column, a tower, a rocket, a stiff corpse, a rising god, a Hermean pillar. The poet here is much the forthrightly demanding male, but sometimes, when he "grasps suddenly the full bud of his vitality," "the gentle garden within her shrinks." As the reader does.

Irony might have saved these poems, but Rilke is rarely ironic. A dash of skepticism, a dollop of sarcasm, could have helped refresh a few of these euphemistic clichés; however—again—Rilke can be angry or contemptuous, but not sarcastic.

If poetry permits the poet to express his feelings and formulate his problems, it can also, quite literally, paper over them: it can toss conflicts into the den of metaphor, where, impossibly, Daniel and the lions mate to produce well-adjusted cubkids.

In Rilke I think women are condemned because women can become mothers. In a Freudian vein (and Rilke learned his Freud from Lou Salomé), Rilke believes the womb to be an ideal place and the world we enter, when we are expelled from it, a foreign and unfriendly realm. In the extraordinary "Eighth Elegy," Rilke produces another one of his continua.

> And yet upon the warm and watchful animal
> there lies the weight and care of an immense sadness.
> Because what often overwhelms us clings to him, too:
> the remembrance that what we reach for now,
> we were once tenderly tethered to. Here all is
> disparity and distance, there it was heartbeat and breath.
> After the first home, our second seems uncertain and
>   cold.
>   Oh the bliss of those so small they can remain in the
>   place where they came to be;
>   Oh the pleasure the midge must know, who will dance
> even its wedding dance in the same world in which it was
>   conceived.
>   Observe the less certain bird, from birth
> almost aware of both, like one of those Etruscan
> souls who has flown the corpse which was its nest,
> yet where its hovering figure still forms the coffin's lid.
>   How confused the bat must be: to come from a womb,
> yet be called upon to fly. As if in flight from itself,

it zigzags through the air like a crack through a cup.
In the same way its wing, at dusk, crazes the porcelain
  surface of the sky.

At the high end of this continuum of self-consciousness is the interior state of Rilke's Angels, creatures who have completed their inwarding and know no change, since in them every change remains. At the low but equally favored end is the insect, who is born, who lives, who dies, in the same world, and knows no wrench. Somewhat worse off is the bird, because, breaking from the egg, which itself needs a nest, it senses, even while it flies, the ultimate difference. Then, in what Theodore Ziolkowski calls Rilke's "weird zoology,"[4] the bat appears, confused because it comes from a womb but is called upon to fly. There are further stages developed in the *Elegies* which Professor Ziolkowski expertly lists: young children, whose self-consciousness is not yet fully realized, and unrequited lovers, whose tender attention to the world has not been narrowed by a beckoning promise, as well as heroes, never sufficiently dipped, and consequently destined to die young.

The poet is just another middle-ager, as alienated, as blinded by interpretation and theory, as every other person—as self-interested and preoccupied as a tradesman—until he takes hold of his self and transforms it into the seer I've spoken of before. Then he becomes (not unlike Our Savior) a mediator between the world which is in constant flight from itself and the glorious, complete, and indifferent Angels.

If we could tell Angels anything, what would we tell them? Is there anything they don't know?

Praise this world to the Angel, not the unutterable one.
You cannot impress him with the splendor you've felt,

for in the heaven of heavens, where he feels so sublimely,
you're but a beginner. Show him some simple thing, then,
that's been changed in its passage through human ages
till it lives in our hands, in the shine of our eyes, as a part
of ourselves. Tell him *things*. He'll stand more astonished,
as you stood by the roper in Rome or the potter in Egypt.
Show him how happy a thing can be, how innocent and
    ours;
how even Sorrow, in the midst of lamenting, is determined
    to alter,
to serve as a thing, or fade in a thing—to escape
into beauty beyond violining.

A billfold. Show the Angel a billfold that has ridden in a rear pocket on someone's rump, the creases it now contains, where money and credit cards once slid in and out, as oiled and stained as a fielder's glove; or a boy's pocketknife, worn short and thin from all those days he's whittled away; or a mohair sofa, shiny where the man wearing that billfold sat, or the cat curled, or love was made.

Could there be a continuum of continua? In any case, here is the beginning of another. At the low end of the scale (and they have no redeeming feature) are the glassine drinking cup, swatches of Kleenex, maybe Band-Aids, objects whose every intention is to disappear into their function; and furthermore, while functioning, to resist becoming in any sense prized or worthy of attention or reuse. Not interesting to any Angel. Next are useful things, such as wrenches, purses, flagons, and so on; which sustain nicks and soils and cracks, stand idle, rust, become as brittle as old bones, break, film with dust; which stay around until they start to show an "expression," and therefore begin to bear, like a stretch of sand, the footprint of a consciousness. Next we arrive at objects created to caress and fondle; to help out our memories: money, of course, silks and satins, dance cards, pillows, a skull, relics and souvenirs, but dolls mostly—the German word is *Puppen*. Things we animate with our feelings. Objects of sentiment, mirrors for our moods. Finally, we reach those items which express an awareness, though they be practical implements, such as newspapers and journals, medical illustrations, cartoons, band music, and those thingamajigs, in addition, which are made merely for amusement: the performances of marionette theaters, for example— puppets, enlivened by the puppeteer's actions, who impose their purely behavioristic life upon their purely passive audience. At last, there are works of art, indicative of the presence of a totally individuated yet universal consciousness concerned solely with ends, and achieving that status for themselves.

In what was to become a notorious essay on dolls that Rilke wrote in the pivotal year of 1914, he differentiates between the doll proper and the marionette (the word in German bears both meanings, as well as a fertile third, "pupa"). The doll's face is fixed, its motion limited, its gaze aimed always in the same way—it is a face of one hardened feeling—nor does it return the hugs or kisses it is given, nor is there resentment if it's tossed. When it functions properly as a doll, it becomes the receptacle for a girlchild's affection, and a player in her daydreams, accompanying her mistress on her trips into imaginary realms. The doll is likely to be treated like a child by the child regardless of the nominally real figure which it represents. The feelings which, like a magnet, the doll attracts hang around it like ghosts, like spiritual frocks, long after it has been set down for the last time and left to live what's left of its leftover life.

The puppet fascinated Rilke. The marionette—stuffed, stringed, hand-worked, mute—is nothing but external appearance, nothing but toddle and mime, a thing among things. The puppet is neither easy nor anxious about being a puppet. The puppet is the hinge between two worlds: that of the puppet master, in whose hands the puppet literally is, and that of the audience it faces; for if the puppet "comes to life" only in performance, it never sees the strings, the moving fingers, or its master's omnipresent eyes. The puppet's success depends upon the illusion of life it generates in its audience. The puppet, with materials as dead as any bolt of cloth or cleverly shaped papier-mâché, and usually shrunken as well, down to dollsize, must mimic the manners (however grotesquely burlesqued) of the audience that watches. They also dance and sing and swing their swords, but they do so because they are alive. The thespian, the hypocrite, the liar, is a feigner, too, but no clever-fingered master makes him act the way he does, or pretend that what is not . . . is, or deny or alter the truth; no, his "acting" is sincere, even if what it pretends to show is not; his desire to deceive comes from inside, it is as meant as cement. One self, removed and hidden, has created another, the self which the world is allowed to see—the idol, the star, the fairy prince.

In a remarkable poem written in Paris in 1907 which its author chose to cut from his first collection of *New Poems*, Rilke displays not only his ambivalence about puppets, but his disapproval of his own psychological makeup. It was an excision for which he never gave a reason, but one which W. L. Graff examines expertly in his *Rainer Maria Rilke: Creative Anguish of a Modern Poet*.[5] It is Graff's opinion that Rilke omitted the poem because it was too revelatory. "Marionettentheater" promptly fell through criticism's cracks, although there was enough evidence elsewhere (in "The Fourth Elegy," in the autobiographical fiction, *Ewald Tragy*, and in the essay on dolls) to suggest the same secret: that Rainer Maria Rilke was Napoleonic, not seraphic.

The poem was occasioned, as Graff points out, by a penitential parade that Rilke witnessed in Furnes, West Flanders. It is a Catholic custom on certain sacred days to carry large statues of saints through the streets (clumsily, in my experience), often in order to reach a pilgrim-like destination, where they'll be ritually placed in order to be properly revered before being returned to base. A robe-end will be made available to be fondled, or kisses will be placed on the back of an indifferently extended plaster hand. Patient queues of the faithful, like the lines at Lenin's tomb, ratchet forward toward the kissing spot, which is wiped after each offering, as loo ladies do, though here by solemn children wielding a rag. But Rilke saw, he thought, two sets of puppets, the statues being carried, and the carriers who were being conned by their faith and manipulated by their priests. This scene became the source of an allegorical poem that refers to more personal matters than he at first realized.

I've made my translation a little freer than elsewhere, partly for clarity's sake, and partly because the poem rhymes (though with reason) relentlessly.

> Behind bars, like beasts,
> they pile up their behavior;
> their voice is not theirs,
> though they swing
> their arms and swords
> with great variety
> as if catching an outcry
> to copy while on the wing.
>
> Their limbs have no joints,
> and hang awkwardly
> in their rig of wires,
> which doesn't prevent them
> from killing or dancing,

or bowing and scraping
like a courtier to a king.

With them, memory has no point;
they wring their awareness dry;
and all they retain inside them
they generally employ
to beat upon their breast
till it's unable to resist.
They know all breasts
are beaten so.

Their large and formal faces
are there for all to see,
simpler than ours, more
forceful and ideal;
open as eyes seem
when awakening from a dream.
A sight which makes laughter
rise from the pit like steam;
for those on the benches see
how the puppets pound,
wound, and frighten one another,
and collapse in loose heaps,
dead of their exertions.
If anyone were to understand it differently,
and fail to laugh at their consternations,
the puppets would replace their play
to reenact a Last Judgment Day.
They would yank on their wires
to pull before the painted porch
the hands that, hidden high above,

had danced them into their desires—
hands hideously red, gloved no longer—
and they would pour from every door,
and climb those wires and cardboard walls
to set their former land afire,
and assassinate those hands.[6]

If, from earliest youth, your inmost self had cried out to escape its circumstances; if you'd looked about and wondered why your presence had been needed even for a moment where you were; and if that meant you had to disappear into an inner distance, leaving your face and figure to fend for themselves, seeking a realm where you could claim an absolute autonomy; if, somewhat to your shame, considering your abject and unaccomplished condition, you had immortal longings in you; if you knew without being told, without having seen any evidence, without therefore knowing, that you were unique, that inside your small delicate body, behind your heavy-lidded eyes, a wide world was contained, and every house there was haunted by dreams, dreams of greatness, ambitions that Ewald Tragy, your namesake, gave away in a petulant moment—"I am my own lawmaker and king," he'd said, "nobody is above me, not even God"—and furthermore, if, to write the great poetry you meant to write, you had first to be a great poet (for where would this sublime stuff come from if not from a sublime soul?), then the fatal division of the self is set; then that hidden ruler must remake both actor and role and push them onto the stage. So his childhood name is eventually altered; so is his handwriting, at Lou Salomé's suggestion, though that is accomplished through the persistent efforts of his will; consequently he must change his nature, change his life; change . . . change . . . with the worry that (in unhappy harmony with his mother's practice) a fine label would not improve the cheap wine that had been decanted down the bottle's slender throat to create a successful deception. Henceforward the poet will be nothing but a Poet, and wander if he must, free to find his inspiration, free to wait for the Muses' touch, despite life's temptations, despite the need for the crowd's applause, because he'll be Orpheus, singing though he seems only a head now, floating downriver in the furious flux of things, for really he'll be whole, head and heart will be at last one. Yet in all this there is the possibility that he'll fail in the role he has assigned himself: which is? that the perfect self (an Angel) must play the part of a perfect appearance (the puppet); in other words, in the first place, that the poetry won't come, and he'll be an ape or a mimic, or, in the second place, that the audience will not be there to applaud, will see the puppet is a puppet, and that, in the third place, the puppet, full of resentment at having lost a normal life for nothing, will turn upon this inside Angel and pull upon his strings, the strings once, solely in his hands, and haul him down from on high (since he's not as on-high as all that, not as perfect as the imagined Angels of the *Elegies*); whereupon the whole show will be over, Doctor Serafico will have failed to heal himself—and there will be no Angel, no poetry, and no poet.

> Erect no memorial stone. Let the rose
> bloom each year just for his sake.
> There Orpheus is. His metamorphosis
> is in this, is this. We don't need to take
>
> on other names. It is always Orpheus
> when there's song. He comes and goes.
> Isn't it enough that he can be with us
> a few days longer than a bowl of roses?

Oh, he has to vanish so you'll know,
though he dreads his disappearance.
Even while his word transcends our souls,

he's already where we cannot go.
The lyre's strings do not bind his hands.
And he obeys while breaking all the bans.[7]

Vindication came that February of 1921, and the inside Angel
and the puppet poet came together in the guise of Orpheus,
who could be called to, who could come, and who did. Rilke felt
an immeasurable relief. Yet, during his career, as he thought
about what he'd written and would write, Rilke realized that if
the puppet, who had sprung into an unpuppetty life to become
a person, had written these poems—not just the *Elegies* he was
struggling to complete, but his entire oeuvre—that puppet-
poet-person could not be Rainer Maria Rilke. Even in his
laments, his singular outcries, as local as their environment was,
as momentary as their occasion, as different from others as his
life; even with these, it could not be Rilke who was writing
them, not if they were going to appeal to the world, not if a
reader was going to be willing to put Rilke's words into his or her
own mouth, to beg the Lord to be allowed to make one single
thing, as if they both were in Spain, at Ronda, in anguish, in
despair.

On July 29, 1920, before the great storm has burst, Rilke
writes to Nanny Wunderly-Volkart: "Ultimately there is only
one poet, that infinite one who makes himself felt, here and
there through the ages, in a mind that can surrender to him." I
have already interpreted Rilke's esthetic position in Kantian
terms, and one could continue that perspective to include even
Ewald Tragy's boast about autonomy, since it could be consid-

ered as a claim to be a noumenal self. "True art," Rilke writes in the fall of that same year, to another correspondent, "can issue only from a purely anonymous center."[8]

If poetry issues from an anonymous center, it certainly gets individualized by the time it reaches the suburbs. Although it is sometimes difficult to tell a cubist painting by Braque from one by Picasso, or a poem by Dryden from a poem by Pope, it is nevertheless generally true that works of art reveal the individuality of the artist in their every brushstroke and semicolon. Where is this anonymous center, especially when we are considering a prototypical Romantic poet? Ewald Tragy says he is unique. "There's no one like me." Rilke might reply that the poet has access to this humanly shared nature, he is not simply governed by it. He can and does sometimes demand an audience, and then he can and sometimes does become its ambassador.

A more compelling reply may be found in the poetry itself. It is not simply at those times when there is a dialogue between Angel and Puppet that the problem of poetry is confronted. It occurs at every intersection: heart roads, lyre strings. And we know that when Rilke issues a command, it is himself he is commanding. Such is the case with the sonnet I call "Dance the Orange."

> Wait . . . that tastes good . . . But already gone.
> . . . A little music now, a tapping, a humming—:
> you girls who are silent, you radiant girls,
> dance the taste of the fruit you are tasting.
>
> Dance the orange. Who can forget it,
> how, drowning in its wealth, it grew
> against its sweetness. You have possessed it,
> as it transforms the delicious into you.

Dance the orange. Fling its sunny clime
from you, so that ripeness may shine
in native breezes. All aglow,

peel perfume from perfume! Share the relation
that the supple pure reluctant rind
has with the juice that fills the joyous fruit.[9]

Wait? There is no waiting room for Time. And fruit, as we know, speaks win and loss into the mouth. Like everything else, the taste is gone before you know it. It is the young women again—*Mädchen*—who are called upon to perform the familiar transformation, whether it is hearing the line that Nature has drawn across our skull, and shivering as though suddenly cold, or out of a bitter taste making wine, or, like Daphne, at her father's wish, turning into a tree, already leafy, awaiting her breeze and the embrace of Apollo. It's not the reputed apple from the tree of knowledge which Adam is somehow handing back to Eve, but the orange—symbol of a rich warm southern life. Dance the sweetness that has become you so that this northern world will feel the sunshine, too. Crucially, the young women are to express the relation between a protective outer appearance and an inner worth.

The rind conceals and protects, but it is not merely an actor, pretending with its peel that the orange is a rock, because the rind is also real. When the poet dies, the praised-over parts of the world, which had become his face because he had so intensely looked at them, will disappear—dissolve to reveal the soft inner core. Rilke, I think, liked to believe that the world he so often watched from a distance, through a window, was a kind of skin, and had its core, too, as he had his. "Ripeness is all" is something he would surely have been willing to repeat, and did, in his own way, often. The poem, too, lets us speak of life and death together—indeed, as he says, in the same breath.

The poem is thus a paradox. It is made of air. It vanishes as the things it speaks about vanish. It is made of music, like us, "the most fleeting of all" yet it is also made of meaning that's as immortal as immortal gets on our mortal earth; because the poem will return, will begin again, as spring returns: it can be said again, sung again, is our only answered prayer; the poem can be carried about more easily than a purse, and I don't have to wait, when I want it, for a violinist to get in key, it can come immediately to mind—to my mind because it is my poem as much as it is yours—because, like a song, it can be sung in many places at once—and danced as well, because the poem becomes a condition of the body, it enlivens our bones, and they dance the orange, they dance the Hardy, the Hopkins, the Valéry, the Yeats; because the poem is a state of the soul, too (the soul we once had), and these states change as all else does, and these states mingle and conflict and grow weak or strong, and even if these verbalized moments of consciousness suggest things which are unjust or untrue when mistaken for statements, when rightly written they are real; they themselves *are* as absolutely as we achieve the Real in this unrealized life—*are*— are with a vengeance; because, oddly enough, though what has been celebrated is over, and one's own life, the life of the celebrant, may be over, the celebration is not over. The celebration goes on.

THE DEATH OF THE POET

He lay. His pillow-propped face could only stare
with pale refusal at the quiet coverlet,
now that the world and all his knowledge of it,

stripped from his senses to leave them bare,
had fallen back to an indifferent year.

Those who had seen him living could not know
how completely one he was with all that flowed;
for these: these deep valleys, each meadowed place,
these streaming waters *were* his face.

Oh, his face embraced this vast expanse,
which seeks him still and woos him yet;
now his last mask squeamishly dying there,
tender and open, has no more resistance,
than a fruit's flesh spoiling in the air.

THE *DUINO ELEGIES* OF
RAINER MARIA RILKE

Among the papers of the
Duchess Marie von Thurn und Taxis-Hohenlohe

THE FIRST ELEGY

Who, if I cried, would hear me among the Dominions
of Angels? And even if one of them suddenly
held me against his heart, I would fade in the grip
of that completer existence—a beauty we can barely
endure, because it is nothing but terror's herald;
and we worship it so because it serenely disdains
to destroy us. Every Angel is awesome.
And so I master myself and stifle the beseeching
heart's cry that's my mating song. Alas, who is there
we can call on? Not Angels, not men,
and even the observant animals are aware
that we're not very happily home here
in this—our interpreted world. Perhaps
some tree on a slope remains for us, allowing our look,
day after day; perhaps yesterday's walk,
and a habit that liked us, like an aging retainer,
loyally stays, and never gives notice.
Oh, then there's Night, when a wind, full of the hollow where
    the world is,
feeds on our faces: who could refuse her,

when she'll gently let us down, though so long longed for
by our heart's solitude? Is she lighter for lovers?
Ah, they only hide their loneliness in one another.
Don't you know that yet? Fling the emptiness out of your arms
to broaden the spaces we breathe—maybe then birds
will feel the amplified air with more fervent flight.

Yes, the springtimes have needed you. There've been stars
to solicit your seeing. In the past, perhaps,
waves rose to greet you, or out an open window,
as you passed, a violin was giving itself
to someone. This was a different commandment.
But could you obey it? Weren't you always
anxiously peering past them, as though
they announced a sweetheart's coming? (Where would you
have hidden her, with those heavy foreign thoughts
tramping in and out and often staying overnight?)

But should you long like this, sing of love's ultimate lovers:
the fame of their feeling is not yet immortal enough.

Those—the forsaken—you envied them almost, they so
        outstripped
all love-appeased lovers in loving. Begin
continually to accomplish their unachievable praise.
Think: the hero endures, even his fading
is a phase of renewal, he burns fresh each day.
But weary Nature gathers back her lovers,
as if she had no second strength to send them forth again.
Have you thought sufficiently of Gaspara Stampa yet,
so that any jilted maiden might, from that more praiseworthy
fashion of loving, feel: can I become like you?
Should not these ancient sorrows finally be

more fruitful for us? Isn't it time that we lovingly
freed ourselves from our lovers and, although shaken,
    endure it,
as the arrow stands in the string to become, upon its
    momentous release,
something more than itself? For staying is nowhere.

Voices, voices. Listen, Oh, my heart, as hitherto only
holy men have listened, listened so the mighty call
lifted them straight from the ground, although they kneeled on,
these magicians—and paid no attention,
they so utterly listened. Not that you could bear
the voice of God—far from it. But hear the flowing
melancholy murmur which is shaped out of silence
wafting toward you now from those youthfully dead.
Whenever you entered a church in Rome or in Naples,
did not their fate speak insistently to you?
or a lofty inscription impose itself upon you
as lately the tablet in Santa Maria Formosa?
What do they want of me? that I should gently cleanse them
of the tarnish of despair which hinders a little,
sometimes, the pure passage of their spirits.

True, it is strange not to live on the earth any longer,
no longer follow the folkways you've only just learned,
not to interpret roses and other promising things
in terms of a rich human future;
then to be no longer the one who once lay
in ceaselessly anxious hands, and to have to put aside
even one's proper name like a broken toy.
Strange, to wish one's wishes no longer. Strange,
to see all that was one time related, fluttering now
loosely in space. And it's difficult to be dead.

There's all that catching up to do before one feels
just a little eternity. All of the living, though,
mistakenly make these knife-like distinctions.
Often Angels (it's said) cannot say if they linger
with the living or the dead. The eternal current
carries every age through either realm
forever, and drowns their voices with its roar in both.

In the end, those taken early no longer need us;
they are tenderly weaned from worldly things,
even as one gently outgrows the breasts of a mother.
But we who have need of such sacred secrets;
we, for whom sorrow's so often the source
of our happiest progress; could *we* survive without them?
Is the legend useless that once, in the lamentation for Linos,
a few adventuresome first notes pierced the barren numbness,
and in the startled space this almost godlike youth
had suddenly forsaken forever, vacancy first felt
the vibration which now carries us, comforts, and helps?[1]

THE SECOND ELEGY

Every Angel is awesome. And yet, alas,
knowing that, I still sing my welcome to you,
almost deadly birds of the soul. Where have the days of Tobias
    gone,
when one of the most fiery-feathered could stand on a simple
    threshold
(disguised for the journey and no longer appalling,
but a youth to the curious youth who peered out).
Yet if the archangel, perilous now, were to step but a step

down toward us from behind the stars, our own heartbeaten
heart would burst our chest. Who *are* you?

Lucky from the cradle, Creation's chosen darlings,
mountain ranges, ridges red from the first sun's rise,
the pollen of a blossoming godhead, crossroads of light,
corridors, staircases, thrones,
space breathed by Being into being, shields of delight, storms
of uninterrupted rapture, and, suddenly, isolate,
mirrors, drawing back, as whole as an echo,
the beauty that has streamed from their face.

But we, when we feel, evaporate; oh, we
breathe ourselves away; from coal to coal
we cool as perfume fades. Though someone may tell us:
"You've got into my blood, into this room, the springtime
is rich with you . . ." What good is that? He can't keep us;
we disappear within, on either side, of him. And those who are
beautiful, who can capture them? Expressions go forth from
        their faces
only to be reabsorbed. Like dew from morning grass
we relinquish what is ours as easily as steam from a warm dish.
O smile, where are you going? O upturned glance:
gone in the glitter of a fresh splash, and its little ripple across
        the heart . . .
nevertheless, that's what we *are*. Does the great world we
        dissolve in
taste of us, then? Do the Angels really
recapture only the radiance that's streamed out from them,
or sometimes, by mischance, is there a bit of our being
brought back? Do we ever figure in their features
even so little as that light vague look

which pregnant women wear? a line not noticed
as they pirouette upon themselves. (Why should they?)

Lovers, if they knew what Angels know, might write
strange words on the night air. For it seems everything
wants to conceal us. Look: trees exist, the houses
we live in still stand. We alone
fly freely by things like loose exchanges of air.
And all conspire to keep quiet about us, partly
out of shame, perhaps, and partly from wordless hope.

Lovers, satisfied by one another, I am asking you
about us. You embrace, but where's the proof?
Look, sometimes it happens that my hands grow to know
one another, or that my weary face seeks their shelter.
This yields me a slender sensation. But who dares to believe he
     exists because of that?
You, though, who from one another's passion
grow until, quite overcome, you plead: "No more . . ."
you, who beneath one another's groping swell
with juice like the grapes of a vintage year;
you, who may go like a bud into another's blossoming:
I am asking you about us. I know
you touch so blissfully because your touch survives such bliss,
because just below your finger's end you feel the tip of pure
     duration.
So you expect eternity to entwine itself in your embrace.
And yet, when you have dealt with your fear of that first look,
the longing, later, at the window, and your first turn
about the garden together: lovers, are you any longer what you
     were?
When you lift yourselves up to one another's lips—chalice to
     chalice—

and slip wine into wine like an added flavor: oh, how strangely
soon is each drinker's disappearance from the ceremony.

On Attic gravestones, did not the discretion in each human
        gesture
amaze you? Weren't love and parting draped
so gently on those shoulders they seemed to be made
of a different stuff from ours? Remember the hands,
how lightly they lay, despite the power in the torsos.
These disciplined figures understood: "We can go no nearer,
this is *our* limit, this tentative touching; the gods can
press confidently down on us, but that is the gods' affair."
If only we could reach something human that's as
pure, modest and secure—a strip of fruitful land
between rock and river. For our heart still
overreaches, as hubris did those others.
And we can no longer follow it into chastening carvings,
or into godlike bodies where its very enhancement
is granted a greater calm.[2]

THE THIRD ELEGY

It is one thing to sing the beloved; another, alas,
to hymn that river god shamefully hid in the blood.
A maiden knows her love like the sky the distant grass.
What does he know of the lord of his lust,
who frequently from loneliness alone raised up
its beaded god-head (even before she's eased him,
and often as though she didn't exist)
to rouse the night into infinite uproar?
O the Neptune aswim in our blood! O his terrible trident!
The dark wind from his chest through the curving conch!

Hear how the night grows hollow as a cave. And you, stars,
is it not from you that the lover's longing for that beloved face
falls? Does not his innermost vision
of her pure features shine to him from your purer fires?

No, neither you, alas! nor his mother
ever bent his brows in such an eager arch;
nor to meet the maiden who enfolds him in her feeling
has his mouth begun to ripen like a fall fruit.
Do you really imagine your light step
so shook him, when your walk is like a waver in the morning
        wind?
Surely you startled his heart; but more primal terrors
overtook him at the shock of your blameless touch.
Call him . . . you can never call him completely from that
        converse
with the dark. Really, he *wants* to, he does escape; relieved,
he starts to feel at home in your heart, accepts and begins to be
        himself.
But could he ever begin himself?
Mother, *you* made him small, it was you who began him,
he was new with you, you arched the friendly world
over those new eyes, and shut the strange outside.
Oh, where are the years, now, when your slender form
stood between him and the drifting chaos of his childhood?
You hid so much from him then; made harmless
the night-frightening room, and sent, from the haven of your
        heart,
a human space like breath into the substance of his dark.
Not in that night, no, but within your nearby Being
you placed a light that shone, as if in friendship, even through
        solid things.

Nowhere the rustle of a stair your smile could not explain,
as though you had long known *when* the floor would choose to
    speak . . .
And he listened and was soothed. So much did your tender
    rising
accomplish; his tall caped fate stepped
behind the wardrobe, and his alarming future,
slightly postponing itself, fit into the folds of the drape.

And he himself—as he lay assuaged, your
delicate image beneath his drowsy lids
dissolving like a sweet in the taste of forthcoming sleep—
seemed safe. But *within* who could divert
or dam the seed-flow of instinct inside him?
Ah, there *was* no caution in that sleeping child; sleeping
but dreaming, but fevered: what he let himself in for!
He, so shy, so untarnished: how interior life entangled
him in its hungry tendrils, its twisted and savage designs,
its constricting embrace, the menacing shapes of its preying
    forms.
How he handed himself over to it —-. Loved.
Loved his inner world, the wilderness inside himself,
that primeval forest from among whose toppled trunks,
accumulated leaves, and silent ruin
rose his pale green heart like a sapling. Loved. Yet left.
Went beyond the place his final roots were rooted to that
    overwhelming origin
where his own little birth was already outlived. Loving,
he descended into his ancestral blood, the ravines
where Gorgons lay gorged like snakes with his fathers.
And every Terror was his pal and winked with complicity.
Yes, Ghastlies smiled at him . . . Seldom

did you, mother, smile so winsomely. *How* could
he not love what smiled such smiles at him? Long before
your love he loved it, for even as you, also swollen, bore him,
it was *there*—dissolved in the fluid that floats the seed.

Look, we don't love like flowers, with only one
springtime behind us; a sap older than memory
mounts in our arms when we love. O my girl,
this: that we've loved, in ourselves, not the one still to come,
but a foaming multitude; not one child alone,
but fathers fallen inside us like the ruins of mountains;
then the dry riverbeds mothers have become;
and the whole of that silent landscape under its clear
or cloudy destiny: *this*, girl, got here ahead of you.

And you yourself, how could you know—that you've
set prehistoric time to ticking in your lover. —What emotions
were exhaled by extinct things. —What women,
through him, hated you. —What sinister men you
vivified in his youthful veins. Dead children
reached out to you . . . Oh, gently, gently,
give him a day's work done with confidence and love. Lead him
nearby a gracious garden; give him restorative nights . . .
                              Hold him in . . . [3]

THE FOURTH ELEGY

O trees of life, when will your winter come?
We're not in tune. Not like migratory birds.
Outmoded, late, in haste, we force ourselves on winds
which let us down upon indifferent ponds.

Reading Rilke

Though we've had to learn how flowering is fading,
somewhere lions still roam,
unaware, in their majesty, of any weakness.

Bent upon one thing, we begin
to feel its burden and the beckon of another.
Hostility's our neighborhood. Aren't lovers
always arriving at the borders of each other,
although both promised breathing space, unimpeded hunting,
    home?
Sometimes a backdrop will be carefully prepared
so that a figure in the foreground
will seem frank and open to us;
but the contours of our feelings stay unknown
when public pressure shapes the face we show.
Who has not sat nervously before his own heart's curtain?
Up it goes: the scene is set for saying farewell.
Easy to understand. The familiar garden
swaying a little before the dancer comes in.
Not *him*. Enough. However elegantly he pretends to move,
he's just a bourgeois in a costume,
and enters his house by the kitchen door.
I will not accept these half-filled masks:
better, a puppet. It's whole. I can endure
the husk it has for body, its wires, its painted face.
Hey! I'm waiting. Even if the lights go out;
even if I'm told, "That's all"; even if absence
drifts toward me like a gray draft from the stage;
even if none of my ancestors will sit silently by me anymore,
nor a woman, nor the boy with the squinting brown eyes:
I'll stay in my seat. One can always watch.

*

Am I not right? You, father, who found life bitter
after you tasted mine, the first infusion of my infant self,
who kept on tasting as my brewing grew,
till, troubled by the aftertaste of such a foreign future,
gazed into my cloudy eyes—you, who, so often
since you died, have lodged your fears about me
deep in my own hopes, giving up that calm
the dead deserve, surrendering a peaceable kingdom
for forebodings about my fate. Am I not right?
and you others, too—am I not right?—who must have loved me
for that first show of love for you I always mislaid
when the look which formed your face,
even as I loved it, became remote as a place in the expanse of
    the world
where you no longer were . . . when I'm inclined
to wait before the puppet stage . . . no,
to stare so intensely as to provoke an Angel to appear,
a player to startle the stuffed skins into life.
Angel and puppet: a real play at last.
Then there comes together like clapping hands
what our being here has pulled apart.
Then the circuit of all cosmic movement can be seen
to arise from the cycle of our seasons.
Then over everything plays the Angel puppeteer.
Surely the dying must sense what a sham it all is,
that nothing is really itself. O hours of childhood,
when behind each shape stood more than the past,
and what lay before us was less than the future.
We grew, and sometimes we wanted to hurry our growing,
partly eager to equal the grown-up
who had for his prize only that.
Yet, when alone, we contented ourselves with what could not
    be clocked.

We stood there in the pause between world and plaything,
in that place which, from the first, had been set aside for a pure
　　　event.

Who'll show a child his proper place? set him among his stars,
and put the measure of earth's distance in his hands?
Who makes the death of a child out of gray bread,
or leaves it there to harden in the round mouth
like the ragged core of a sweet apple? Murderers
aren't hard to understand. But this: to hold death,
the whole of death, even before one's life's begun,
to hold it gently, without complaint:
this exceeds description.[4]

THE FIFTH ELEGY
Dedicated to Frau Hertha Koenig

But tell me, who are they, these troupers,
even more transient than we are—driven since childhood,
and bent (for what? for whom?) by some tireless will?
Because it wrings them, twists them, swings and flings them,
tosses and catches them; and they descend
as if the air were oiled and polished,
to light on a carpet worn threadbare
by their incessant leaping and landing,
a carpet lost in cosmic space.
Stuck there like a bandage, as if the suburban sky
had bruised the earth.

　　　　　　　　　　　　　　　　　And barely there,
upright, displayed there, the great first letter of
Da . . . for in Fate's repeated and relentless grip
even the strongest men are tossed, in whim,

from their station again, the way Augustus the Strong
toyed with the tin platter that served his table.

Ah, and around this center,
attention like a rose
blooms and sheds its petals. About this
pestle-like pistil, its surface shining with sham and smirk;
impregnated by its own pollen
so it bears boredom's seedless fruit.

There's the weary and wrinkled weight lifter,
able only, so old, to beat a drum,
shrunk in his scrotum-like skin
as if it had once held two men,
though now one's dead in the ground
while he lives on, deaf and dazed
in his widower's weeds.

Then the young one, the man, who might be
the son of a neck and a nun,
tense and tightly filled
with muscle and simplicity.
Oh, and you, to be the plaything of some pain,
while it was still little, a gift
during one of its long convalescences . . .

You, who fall with the thud
only green fruit know,
like daily rain from the tall boughs
the movements of your troupe create
(a tree which passes through its seasons
more rapidly than water, spring to fall),
only to land where your grave will be.

Reading Rilke

Sometimes, in a momentary pause, you
feel a shy look of love, for one seldom allowed to be your
     mother,
begin to flood your face, though it will soon be
absorbed by the business of your body.
Again, the man's clapping hands are calling for more leaping,
but before an honest anguish can catch up
with your racing heart—
the true source of painful feeling—
comes the sting in the soles of your feet,
to force its few tears from your eyes.
Yet there's that blind smile.
Angel! Oh, take that smile! pluck that little flowered herb of
     healing,
find a vase to save it! Include it among those joys
not yet open to us. In a graceful urn
let an ornate inscription praise it: "Subrisio Saltat."

You, then, lovely one,
you, over whom the most enchanting pleasures
have skipped without a sound,
maybe your fringes are happy for you,
or the green metallic silk
that binds your firm full breasts
feels itself so soothed it needs nothing further.

You,
lifted upon shoulders to be shown,
and balanced and rebalanced on swaying scales,
calmly, like a marketed fruit.

Where, oh, where, is that place—I bear in my heart—
so long a way from hard-earned mastery,

where they fell away from one another like mating animals,
weary, ill-matched,
where weights were too heavy,
where their spinning plates
still toppled from the tips of their futilely stirring sticks . . . ?

Suddenly, in this tiresome no-man's-land, suddenly,
in this indescribable place, the always "not good enough"
is magically transformed—turns back to start,
and into a sterile perfection
where the long-columned bill
adds up and adds up . . . adds up to nil.

Squares, O square in Paris, ceaseless showplace,
where the *modiste* Madame Lamort
weaves and winds the restless ways of the world,
those endless ribbons, into ever new designs:
bows, frills, flowers, cockades, artificial fruit,
each cheaply dyed, to decorate
the tacky winter hats of Fate.
. . . .
Angel: if there were a place we knew nothing of,
and there, on some mystical carpet, the lovers did everything
that's unachievable here—showed their somersaulting souls,
hearts' leaps, their towered palaces of pleasure,
ladders a long time leaning in a tremble against one another
on no more ground than cloud—
suppose they could dare to do it all there,
in front of the silent, the numberless dead:
    Would these spectators, then, toss down
their savings, their hidden and unknown hoard,
their still legal coins of happiness

at the feet of that genuinely smiling couple,
and upon that now gratified carpet?[5]

THE SIXTH ELEGY

Fig tree, for a long time it has meant much to me
how you almost forget to flower,
and then, without fanfare, force your concentrated essence
into the season's first fruit.
Like the tube of a fountain, your arching boughs
circulate the sap, driving it down and then up,
till it leaps from sleep, though still drowsy,
into the outburst of its sweetest achievement.
Like that god gone into swan.

                         . . . But we linger,
alas, we boast about our blooming; already betrayed,
we reach the core of our fruit too late.
In a few the impulse to action is so powerful
that when the temptation to bloom lightly touches
their young mouths, their lowered eyelids,
like evening air, they are instantly tumescent:
heroes, perhaps, and those who've been chosen
to disappear early, whose veins the gardener of souls
has fastened like vines to a different lattice.
They race ahead of their own laughter
the way the triumphant king's team precedes him
in those slowly receding reliefs at Karnak.

The hero strangely resembles those who die
in their youth.

                      Survival doesn't concern him.

Rising composes his Being. He takes himself
on always perilous journeys into the changing
constellations of his far-off stars. Where few
could find him. But Fate, mum about us,
as if inspired, suddenly sings him like a bird
borne into the buffets of a storm. For I hear no one like *him*.
On an aroused wind, his dark song rushes through me.
    Also, I would love to hide from my longings:
oh, to be a boy again, my life ahead,
to sit propped on my future arms and read
about Samson—how at first his mother
was barren, and then bore all.

Within you, O Mother, was he not a hero already,
didn't his imperious choice begin there, inside you?
Thousands were stirring in that womb and wanting to be what
    he was.
But see: he chose and selected, he seized and used.
And if he ever pushed columns apart, it was when
he burst from the world of your body
into that temple of enemies called the world,
where he went on choosing and doing.
Oh, mothers of heroes, oh sources of raging rivers;
and you ravines into which sorrowing maidens, from the heart's
    edge, have already plunged—
former and future victims of your son!
    For even as the Hero overcame the labors and trials of love,
the hearts that beat harder on his behalf
could only lift him above all his obstacles,
until, already beginning to turn his back, he stood
at the end of these many smiles, another self.[6]

THE SEVENTH ELEGY

No more courting. Voice, you've outgrown seduction.
It can't be the excuse for your song anymore,
although you sang as purely as a bird
when the soaring season lifts him, almost forgetting
he's just an anxious creature, and not a single heart
that's being tossed toward brightness, into a home-like heaven.
No less than he, you'd be courting some silent companion
so she'd feel you, though you're perched out of sight,
some mate in whom a reply slowly wakens
and warms in her hearing—your ardent feeling finding a fellow
    flame.

Oh, and springtime would understand—there'd be
no corner that wouldn't echo with annunciation.
First each little questioning note
would be surrounded by a confident day's magnifying stillness.
Then the intervals between calls, the steps rising toward the
    anticipated temple
of what's to come; then the trill, the way a fountain's
falling is caught by its next jet as though in play . . .
With the summer ahead.
   Not only all of summer's dawns, the way they
shine before sunrise and dissolve into day.
Not only the days, so soft around flowers, and above,
shaping the trees, so purposeful and strong.
Not only the devotion of these freed forces,
not only the paths, not only meadows at evening,
not only the ozoned air after late thunder,
not only, at dusk, the onset of sleep and twilight's
    premonitions . . .

but also the nights! the height of summer nights,
and the stars as well, the stars of the earth.
Oh, to be dead someday so as eternally to know them,
all the stars: then how, how, how to forget them!

Look, I've been calling my lover, but not only she would
    come . . .
Out from their crumbling graves girls would rise and gather.
How could I confine my call—once called—to just one?
Like seeds, the recently interred are always seeking the earth's
    surface.
My children, one thing really relished in this world
will serve for a thousand. Never believe
that destiny is more than what's confined to a childhood;
how often did you pass the man you loved, panting,
panting after the blissful chase, to dash into freedom?

It is breathtaking simply to be here. Girls, even you
knew, who seemed so deprived, so reduced, who became
sewers yourselves, festering in the awful alleys of the city.
For each of you had an hour, perhaps a bit less,
at worst a scarcely measurable span between while and while,
when you wholly *were*. Had all. Were bursting with Being.
But we easily forget what our laughing neighbor
neither confirms nor envies. We want to show it off,
yet the most apparent joy reveals itself only after
it has been transformed, when it rises *within* us.
    My love, the world exists nowhere but within us.
Withinwarding is everything. The outer world
dwindles, and day fades from day. Where once
a solid house was, soon some invented structure
perversely suggests itself, as at ease among ideas
as if it still stood in the brain.

The Present has amassed vast stores of power,
shapeless as the vibrant energy it has stolen from the earth.
It has forgotten temples. We must save in secret
such lavish expenditures of spirit.
Yes, even where one thing we served, knelt for, and
prayed to survives, it seeks to see itself invisible.
Many have ceased perceiving it, and so will miss
the chance to enlarge it, add pillars and statues, give it
     grandeur, within.

   Each torpid turn of the world disinherits some
to whom neither what's been nor will be adheres.
For to humans even what comes next is far away.
We, however, should not be confused by this,
but should resolve to retain the shape in stone we still
     recognize.
This once stood like a standard among mankind,
stood facing fate, the destroyer, stood in the middle
of our not knowing what, why, or wherefore, as though an
     answer existed,
and took its design from the stars' firm place in heaven.
Angel, to you I shall show it—there! in your eyes
it shall stand seen and redeemed at last, straight
as pillars, pylons, the sphinx, the cathedral's
gray spire thrust up from a decaying or a foreign city.

Wasn't it miraculous? O marvel, Angel, that we *did it*,
we, O great one, extol our achievements,
my breath is too short for such praise.
Because, after all, we haven't failed to make use
of our sphere—*ours*—these generous spaces.
(How frightfully vast they must be,
not to have overflowed with our feelings

even after these thousands of years.)
But one tower was great, wasn't it? O Angel, it was—
even compared to you? Chartres was great—
and music rose even higher, flew far beyond us.
Even a woman in love, alone at night by her window . . .
didn't she reach your knee?

                Don't think I'm courting you, Angel.
And even if I were! You'd never come.
For my call is always full of "stay away."
Against such a powerful current even you cannot advance.
My call is like an outstretched arm. And its upturned,
open, available hand is always in front of you,
yet only to ward off and warn,
though wide open, incomprehensible.[7]

THE EIGHTH ELEGY
Dedicated to Rudolf Kassner

All other creatures look into the Open
with their whole eyes. Our eyes, instead, go round the other
    way,
setting snares and traps on every path to freedom.
What *is* outside, we read solely from the animal's gaze,
for we compel even the young child to turn and look back at
    preconceived things,
never to know the acceptance so deeply set inside
the animal's face. Free from death.
It is all we see. The free animal
always has its decline behind, its god ahead,
and when it moves, it moves within eternity the way fountains
    flow.
We've never had that sort of pure space before us,

into which flowers endlessly open—no, not for a single day—
there's always the interpreted world, and even our
abstract realms reflect a repeated yes or no:
never that pure unmonitored element one breathes,
naturally knows, and never craves. As a child
one may be absorbed by silence only to be shaken
out of it again. Or one dies and *is* it.
Too close to death, one may see it no longer,
to stare ahead instead, maybe with the wide eyes of animals.
Lovers approach it, and would be amazed,
were not a partner always in the way . . .
It opens up behind the other almost by mistake . . .
but no one gets beyond the other, and the world comes back
    again.
Continuously confronted by creation, we see there
only a dimmed reflection of the free and open.
Or some dumb animal, with its calm eyes,
is seeing through and through us.
That's our Fate, to be possessed by the opposite,
to see an inversion and nothing more.

If this confident creature coming toward us,
on such a different course, had our kind of consciousness,
he would spin us around and drag us in his wake.
But to him he is infinite, incomprehensible,
and because he is blind to his condition,
his outward gaze is pure. Where we see
the future, he sees all, and sees himself in everything,
he and all, whole always.

And yet upon the warm and watchful animal
there lies the weight and care of an immense sadness.
Because what often overwhelms us clings to him, too:

the remembrance that what we reach for now,
we were once tenderly tethered to. Here all is
disparity and distance, there it was heartbeat and breath.
After the first home, our second seems uncertain and cold.
  Oh, the bliss of those so small they can remain in the place
    where they came to be;
Oh, the pleasure the midge must know, who will dance
even its wedding dance in the same world in which it was
    conceived.
Observe the less certain bird, from birth
almost aware of both, like one of those Etruscan
souls who has flown the corpse which was its nest,
yet where its hovering figure still forms the coffin's lid.
How confused the bat must be: to come from a womb,
yet be called upon to fly. As if in flight from itself,
it zigzags through the air like a crack through a cup.
In the same way its wing, at dusk, crazes the porcelain surface
    of the sky.

And we: spectators always, everywhere,
looking on, but never beyond!
World overwhelms us. We order it. The order falls.
We rearrange it and come apart ourselves.

Who has turned us around like this,
so that whatever we do, we wear the look of someone
    departing?
As he who halts, one final time,
on a hill high enough
to show off his whole valley,
wavers and stops and lingers there,
we too live our lives forever taking leave.[8]

THE NINTH ELEGY

Why, if the seasons of life could be passed
as a laurel, a little darker than all other green,
with tiny waves on the edge of each leaf,
like the smile of a wind—: why, then,
must we be human—and, shunning our Destiny,
long for Fate? . . .
                                        Oh, not because happiness—
that profit snatched hastily from threatening loss—
exists: not from curiosity, not simply to practice
a heart that could live quite as well in a laurel . . .
but because it is much just to be here,
because all that is fleeting here needs us,
strangely concerns us. Us, most fleeting of all.
Just *once*. Everything. Only *once*. *Once* and no more.
And we as well: *once*. Then never again. But this
having *been* once, although *only* once,
having been earthed—can it ever be canceled?

And so we push ourselves on and pray to achieve it,
to hold it in our simple hands,
in our ever more crowded gaze, in our speechless heart.
Pray to become it. To give it to someone? We'd rather
keep it a keepsake forever . . . But to that other land,
alas, what can be taken? Not our power of perceiving,
learned here so slowly; nothing here that's happened.
Nothing. But possibly suffering. Above all, the hardness of life,
and the long endurance of love—wholly
untellable things. But later, when the stars have us under them,
what then is the use? The stars are still better unspoken.
Nor does the wanderer bring down a handful of earth

from his high mountain slope to the valley (for earth, too, is
     mute),
but a word he has plucked from the climbing: the yellow and
     blue
gentian. Are we, perhaps, *here* just to utter: house,
bridge, fountain, gate, jug, fruit tree, window—
at most: column, tower . . . but to *utter* them, remember,
to speak in a way which the named never dreamed
they could *be*? Isn't it the hidden purpose
of this cunning earth, in urging on lovers,
to realize, through their rapture, rapture for all?
Threshold: what it can mean for two lovers
to foot down their threshold a little,
just as the many who've come through have worn it,
and ahead of the many to follow . . . so lightly.

Here is the time for words, *here* is its home.
Speak and proclaim. More than ever,
the things we can live with are falling away,
and imageless action's usurping their place.
Real acts will quickly crack their shells
when what's working within them
brings forth a new form.

Our heart dwells between hammers,
like the tongue between the teeth,
where it remains, notwithstanding,
a continual creator of praise.

Praise this world to the Angel, not the unutterable one.
You cannot impress *him* with the splendor you've felt,
for in the heaven of heavens, where he feels so sublimely,
you're but a beginner. Show him some simple thing, then,

that's been changed in its passage through human ages
till it lives in our hands, in the shine of our eyes, as a part
of ourselves. Tell him *things*. He'll stand more astonished,
as you stood by the roper in Rome or the potter in Egypt.
Show him how happy a thing can be, how innocent and ours;
how even Sorrow, in the midst of lamenting, is determined to
    alter,
to serve as a thing, or fade in a thing—to escape
into beauty beyond violining. These things whose life
is a constant leaving, they know when you praise them.
Transient, they trust us, the most transient, to come
to their rescue; they wish us to alter them utterly,
within our invisible hearts, into—so endlessly—us!
Whoever we may finally be.

   You earthly things—is this not what you want,
to arise invisible in us? Is not your dream
to be one day invisible? Earth!—things!—invisible!
What, if not this deep translation, is your ardent aim?
Earth, my loved one, I will. Believe me.
You need no more of your springtimes to win me.
Already one is more than my blood can endure.
Beyond all the words I can speak I am yours,
as I've been from the beginning. Always, you were right,
and your holiest thought's been of death, our most intimate
    friend.
But look—I live. Oh, on what? Neither childhood nor
future grows less. Abundant existence
wells up in my heart.[9]

THE TENTH ELEGY

Someday, released at last from this anguished soul-searching,
may I sing an extolling song to the assenting Angels;
may not even one of the firmly struck hammers of the heart
land upon a slack, uncertain, or broken string;
may my weeping face make me more radiant,
each tear glistening like a new bloom:
how precious to me then my tormented nights will be, and how
    deep my regret
that I didn't more willingly kneel to you,
inconsolable sisters, more willingly lose myself in your flowing
    hair.
We squander our sorrows. How we look along their bitter
    lengths
searching for an end, and see not their secret.
But they are our serious winter trees, our dark evergreens,
one season of our inner year—not just a season,
but soil, place, village, storehouse, home.

Yet, alas, how strange are the streets of the City of Pain,
where, amid the noise raised against noise that we mistake for
    stillness,
a stout figure swaggers, cast in inanities' mold:
itself the gilded din, and decaying memorials.
Oh, how completely would an Angel crush underfoot their
    market of cheap comforts,
with the church at its side, purchased ready-made,
as swept, as shut, as disappointing as a post office on a Sunday.
The outskirts, though, are always swirling with carnival.
Elevating swings! Daring jugglers and exciting High Divers!

And the shooting galleries with their lifelike ducks,
targets which will fall in a clatter of tin
when a lucky shot happens to hit one.
Encouraged by the crowd, he waddles after more prizes:
booths that can satisfy any kind of curiosity
are drumming their drums and crying their wares.
Especially worth seeing, but for adults only: coins in
    copulation,
right there onstage, money's metal genitals rubadubdubbing.
Educational, and sure to encourage multiplication . . .
                                       Oh, and
just outside that tent, behind the last billboards,
plastered with posters for "Todlos,"
the dark bitter beer so sweet to the addicted,
so long as they swallow it while chewing on fresh distractions—
and just at the back of the billboards, right behind them, is . . .
    reality.
Children are playing; to one side, earnest,
in patchy grass, lovers are holding each other,
and dogs are doing nature's business.
The young man is drawn farther on; perhaps he loves a young
    Lament . . .
He follows her into the meadows. She says:
We live out there. A long way . . .
Where? And the young man follows. He's moved by her
    manner: her shoulders, her neck—
maybe she comes from a noble family? Still, he leaves her,
turns back, looks around, waves . . . What's the use?
She's a Lament.

Only those who died young, in their first stages
of timeless serenity, scarcely weaned,

follow her lovingly. She waits and befriends the girls.
Gently shows them what she's wearing. Pearls
the shape of tears, and patience's fine-spun veils.
She walks with the young men in silence.

But there in the valley where they live,
one of the older Laments answers the youth's questions:
Long ago, she says, the Lamentations were a powerful clan.
Our fathers worked the mines in that mountain range.
Among humans, sometimes, you can still find a polished lump
    of primal pain,
or a piece of petrified rage amid the slag of an ancient volcano.
Yes, that would have come from there. We used to be rich.

   And gently she guides him through the immense land of
    Lamentation,
shows him temple columns or the ruins of castles
where the Lords of Lamentation wisely ruled
the country long ago. Shows him the tall weeping trees,
shows him fields flowering with griefstrife
(which the living only know as becalmed leaves);
shows him sorrow's pastured herds—and sometimes
a startled bird, cutting across their gaze,
loops the first letter of its lonely cry.
At evening she leads him to the graves of the elders,
the seers and sybils who prophesied and warned.
But with night coming on, they move more slowly,
and soon the tomb, whose stone, awash with
moonlight, rises to watch over all, confronts them.
Brother to the Nile's sublime Sphinx, the silent chamber's
    secret face.
And they are stunned by the crowned head that has quietly
    formed—

forever—the features of man
on the scale of the stars.

His eyes can't take it in, his mind still reeling from recent
    death,
but their gaze frightens an owl from behind the stone crown.
And the bird, with slow swooping strokes, brushes the statue's
    fuller cheek
until that touching faintly speaks,
in death's different hearing,
as though on the facing pages of an open book
an unutterable shape were shaped.

And higher, the stars. New ones. The stars of Pain's Land.
Slowly the Lament names them: "There, look:
there's the *Rider*, the *Staff*, and they call that bigger
constellation *Garland of Fruit*. Then, farther on,
toward the Pole: *Cradle, Path, Puppet, Window, The Burning
    Book*.
But in the southern sky, clear as lines on the palm of a blessed
    hand,
the brilliantly glowing 'M'
that stands for Mothers . . . "

But the dead youth must go on, and silently the elder Lament
leads him as far as the gorge
where the true Source of Joy
shines in the moonlight.
Solemnly she names it and says: "For men
it is the stream which bears them on."

They stand at the foot of the range,
and there she embraces him, weeping.

Alone he climbs the Mountains of Primal Pain.
And not once does his step echo from
Destiny's soundless path.

Yet if the eternal dead were to wake an image in us,
look, they might be pointing to the catkins
hanging from empty hazels, or they might remind us
of the rain that falls on the dark earth in early spring.

And we, who have always thought
of happiness as *ascending*,
would feel the emotion
that almost undoes us
when a happy thing *falls*.[10]

NOTES

Lifeleading

1. *Life of a Poet: Rainer Maria Rilke,* by Ralph Freedman. New York: Farrar, Straus and Giroux, 1995, 129.
2. Cambridge: Cambridge Univ. Press, 1941; reprinted by Octagon Books, New York: Octagon Books Farrar, Straus and Giroux, 1971. More recently (1988), Peter Lang has published Beatrice Bullock-Kimball's monograph, *The European Heritage of Rose Symbolism and Rose Metaphors in View of Rilke's Epitaph.*
3. Capri, ca. New Year's Day 1907.
4. Paris, June 27, 1906.
5. *My Sister, My Spouse: A Biography of Lou Andreas-Salomé.* New York: Norton and Co., 1962, new ed. 1974, 186, 270.
6. New York: Fromm Intl., 1984, 73.
7. *Rilke: A Life,* by Wolfgang Leppmann. New York: Fromm International, 1984, 75.
8. Freedman, *Life of a Poet,* 113.
9. Quoted by H. F. Peters in *Rainer Maria Rilke: Masks and the Man.* Seattle: Univ. of Washington Press, 1960. Reprinted by Gordian Press, NY, 1977, 10.
10. Freedman, *Life of a Poet,* 373.
11. "Parting," Paris, early 1906.
12. From "The Book of Poverty and Death," which is Book III of *The Book of Hours,* 1903.
13. From "Turning-Point," Paris, 1914.
14. "Autumn," Paris, Sept. 11, 1902.

Notes

15. "Autumn Day," Paris, Sept. 21, 1902.
16. New York: Farrar, Straus and Giroux, 1996.
17. "To Music," a gift to Frau Hanna Wolff after a private concert at her home, Munich, Jan. 11 or 12, 1918.
18. "The Lace," II, Capri, ca. Feb. 10, 1907.
19. "Buddha," Meudon, end of 1905.
20. *Phases of Rilke*, Bloomington: Indiana Univ. Press, 1958, 72.
21. *The Romantic Rebellion*, New York: Harper and Row, 1973, 353, 4.
22. "The Panther," Jardin des Plantes, Paris, 1903.
23. From "The Fourth Elegy."
24. Last entry in Rilke's pocket book, Val-Mont, Switzerland, mid-December 1926.

Transreading

1. Meudon, Winter 1905–6.
2. See Michael Hamburger's "Brief Afterthoughts on Versions of a Poem by Hölderlin," in *Translating Poetry*, edited by Daniel Weissbort. Iowa City: Univ. of Iowa Press, 1989, 51–6.
3. *Rilke's Book of Hours*, 111.
4. II.7 of "The Book of Pilgrimage" from *The Book of Hours*.

Ein Gott Vermags

1. Reprinted in the *Canadian Review of Comparative Literature* VII, no. 2, 1980, 163–73.
2. Arndt, *The Best of Rilke*, 162.
3. *Sonnets to Orpheus*, Part I, 3, Muzot, Feb. 2–5, 1922.
4. *Sonnets to Orpheus*, Part I, 1, Muzot, Feb. 2–5, 1922.
5. *Sonnets to Orpheus*, Part I, 2, Muzot, Feb. 2–5, 1922.
6. *Sonnets to Orpheus*, Part II, 13, Muzot, Feb. 15–17, 1922.
7. Vol. 2, *Poetry*, 143.
8. "Torso of an Archaic Apollo," Paris, early Summer 1908, in *New Poems*, Part II.

Notes

Inhalation in a God

1. *The Poems of Alexander Pope,* a one-volume edition of the Twickenham text, edited by John Butt. New Haven: Yale Univ. Press, 1963, 265.
2. "Lament," Paris, July 1914.
3. From "The Ninth Elegy."
4. "The Spanish Trilogy," I, Ronda, Jan. 6, 1913.
5. Quotations are from "Mathematical Creation," in *The Creative Process,* edited by Brewster Ghiselin. Berkeley: Univ. of California Press, 1952, 33–42.
6. "The Great Night," Paris, 1914.

Schade

1. Freedman, *Life of a Poet,* 155.
2. *Paula Modersohn-Becker,* by Gillian Perry. New York: Harper & Row, 1979, 126, plate xvi.
3. Freedman, *Life of a Poet,* 266.
4. Paula Modersohn-Becker, *The Letters and Journals,* Günter Busch and Liselette von Reinken, eds.; Arthur S. Wensinger and Carole Clew Hoey, trans. Evanston, Ill.: Northwestern Univ. Press, 1990, 195.
5. From "Requiem for a Friend."
6. Modersohn-Becker, *Letters and Journals,* 539.
7. Ibid., 540.
8. Freedman, *Life of a Poet,* 254.
9. Paris, Oct. 31–Nov. 2, 1908.

The Grace of Great Things

1. "Primal Sound," in G. Craig Houston, trans., *Rainer Maria Rilke, Selected Works,* vol. I, *Prose,* 51–6.
2. Quoted in *My European Heritage,* by Brigitte B. Fischer. Boston: Brandon Publishing, 1986, 76.
3. *Sonnets to Orpheus,* Part II, 1, Feb. 23, 1921.
4. *Sonnets to Orpheus,* Part II, 29, Feb. 19–23.

5. From "The Ninth Elegy."
6. From "The First Elegy."
7. London: Chatto and Windus, 1972.
8. *Sonnets to Orpheus,* Part II, 12, Muzot, Feb. 15–17, 1922.
9. Paris, mid-July 1906.
10. Rilke, in a letter to Hermann Pongs, quoted by Leppmann, 183.
11. From "The Fifth Elegy."
12. From "The Fourth Elegy."
13. *Sonnets to Orpheus,* Part I, 13.
14. "Transformations," quoted by Martin Seymour Smith in *Hardy.* London: Bloomsbury, 1994, 31.
15. From "The Fourth Elegy."
16. Paris, June 20, 1914.
17. From "The Ninth Elegy."
18. *Sonnets to Orpheus,* Part II, 29.
19. Greene and Norton, *Letters of Rainer Maria Rilke,* vol. 2, 1910–26, 139–40.
20. "Death," Munich, November 9, 1915.
21. From "The Seventh Elegy."

Erect No Memorial Stone

1. *"Oh sage, Dichter, was du tust?"* December 1921. Inscribed in a copy of *Malte Laurids Brigge* belonging to Leonie Zacharias.
2. "Man Must Die Because He Has Known Them" from the sayings of Ptah-hotep, ms. from ca. 2000 B.C. Paris, July 1914.
3. Norton: New York, 1975.
4. In *The Classical German Elegy 1795–1950,* Princeton, N.J.: Princeton Univ. Press, 1980, 242.
5. Princeton, N.J.: Princeton Univ. Press, 1956, 295–333.
6. "Puppet Theater," Paris, July 20, 1907.
7. *Sonnets to Orpheus,* Part I, 5, Muzot, Feb. 2–5, 1921.
8. Quoted by Mitchell in the excellent notes to his translation, *The Sonnets to Orpheus,* 164.
9. *Sonnets to Orpheus,* Part I, 15, Muzot, Feb. 2–5, 1921.

The *Duino Elegies* of Rainer Maria Rilke

1. Schloss Duino, Jan. 21, 1912.
2. Schloss Duino, late Jan.–early Feb. 1912.
3. Begun at Schloss Duino early in 1912; continued and completed in Paris, late Autumn 1913.
4. Munich, Nov. 22 and 23, 1915.
5. Château de Muzot, Sierre, Switzerland, Feb. 14, 1922.
6. Lines 1–31, Ronda, Spain, Jan.–Feb. 1913; lines 42–44, Paris, late Autumn 1913; lines 32–41, Château de Muzot, Feb. 9, 1922.
7. Château de Muzot, Feb. 7, 1922.
8. Château de Muzot, Feb. 7–8, 1922.
9. The first six lines, Schloss Duino, March 1912; the remainder, Château de Muzot, Feb. 9, 1922.
10. Lines 1–12 at Schloss Duino, Jan.–Feb. 1912; continued in Paris during late Autumn 1913; a new conclusion, lines 13 to the end, at Château de Muzot, Feb. 11, 1922.

BIBLIOGRAPHY

Translations of the *Elegies* in Order of Publication

Duineser Elegien. Elegies from the Castle of Duino, translated by V. Sackville West. London: The Hogarth Press, 1931.

Duino Elegies, translated by J. B. Leishman and Stephen Spender. New York: Norton, 1939.

Sonnets to Orpheus. Duino Elegies, translated by Jessie Lamont. New York: Fine Editions Press, 1945.

Duineser Elegien. The Elegies of Duino, translated by Nora Wydenbruck. Vienna: Amandus, 1948.

The Duino Elegies, translated by Harry Behn. Mount Vernon, N.Y.: Peter Pauper Press, 1957.

Rainer Maria Rilke, Selected Works, vol. 2, *Poetry,* translated by J. B. Leishman. Norfolk, Conn.: New Directions, 1960.

Duino Elegies, translated by C. F. MacIntyre. Berkeley and Los Angeles: Univ. of California Press, 1961.

The Duino Elegies, translated by Stephen Garmey and Jay Wilson. New York: Harper & Row, 1972.

Duinesian Elegies, translated by Elaine E. Boney. Chapel Hill: Univ. of North Carolina Press, 1975.

Duino Elegies and the Sonnets to Orpheus, translated by A. Poulin, Jr. Boston: Houghton Mifflin, 1977.

Duino Elegies, translated by David Young. New York: Norton, 1978.

Duino Elegies, translated by Gary Miranda. Portland, Oreg.: Breitenbush Books, 1981.

Bibliography

The Selected Poetry of Rainer Maria Rilke, edited and translated by Stephen Mitchell. New York: Random House, 1982.

Rainer Maria Rilke, Selected Poems [including the first, fourth, fifth, sixth, and tenth *Elegies*], translated by Albert Ernest Flemming. 2nd expanded edition, New York: Methuen, 1985.

Duino Elegies, translated by Robert Hunter. Eugene, Oreg.: Hulogos'i Communications, 1987.

Rilke. Duino Elegies, translated by Stephen Cohn. Manchester, England: Carcanet, 1989.

The Duino Elegies, translated by Louis Hammer and Sharon Ann Jaeger. Old Chatham, N.Y.: Sachem Press, 1991.

Duino Elegies, translated by David Oswald. Einsiedeln, Switzerland: Daimon Verlag, 1992.

Translations of the *Sonnets to Orpheus*

Sonnets to Orpheus, translated with notes and commentary by J. B. Leishman. London: The Hogarth Press, 1936.

Sonnets to Orpheus, translated by M. D. Herter Norton. New York: Norton and Co., 1942.

Sonnets to Orpheus. Duino Elegies, translated by Jessie Lamont. New York: Fine Editions Press, 1945.

Sonnets to Orpheus, translated by C. F. MacIntyre. Berkeley: Univ. of California Press, 1960.

Duino Elegies and the Sonnets to Orpheus, translated by A. Poulin, Jr. Boston: Houghton Mifflin, 1977.

Sonnets to Orpheus, translated by Charles Haseloff. Privately printed. Brooklyn: The Print Center, 1979.

The Sonnets to Orpheus, translated by Kenneth Pitchford. Harrison, N.Y.: The Purchase Press, 1981.

The Sonnets to Orpheus, translated by Stephen Mitchell, with notes and variants. New York: Simon and Schuster, 1985.

Bibliography

Translations of the *New Poems* Only

New Poems, translated, with notes and introduction, by J. B. Leishman. London: The Hogarth Press, 1964.

New Poems [1907], translated by Edward Snow. San Francisco: North Point Press, 1984.

New Poems: The Other Part [1908], translated by Edward Snow. San Francisco: North Point Press, 1987.

Selections and Other Volumes of Poetry

The Best of Rilke, translated by Walter Arndt, with a foreword by Cyrus Hamlin. Hanover, N.H.: Univ. Press of New England, 1989.

The Book of Fresh Beginnings: Selected Poems of Rainer Maria Rilke, translated with an introduction by David Young. Oberlin, Ohio: Field Translation Series, 20, 1994.

The Book of Hours, translated by A. L. Peck, with an introduction by Eudo Mason. London: The Hogarth Press, 1961.

The Book of Images, translated by Edward Snow. San Francisco: North Point Press, 1991.

Correspondence in Verse with Erika Mitterer, translated by N. B. Cruickshank, with an introduction by J. B. Leishman. London: The Hogarth Press, 1953.

Fifty Selected Poems, translated by C. F. MacIntyre. Berkeley: Univ. of California Press, 1940. [The 2nd ed., 1941, is called *Translations from Rilke.*]

From the Remains of Count C.W., translated with an introduction by J. B. Leishman. London: The Hogarth Press, 1952.

The Lay of the Love and Death of the Cornet Christopher Rilke, translated by Leslie Phillips and Stefan Schimanski. London: Lindsay Drummond, 1948.

The Lay of the Love and Death of the Cornet Christopher Rilke, translated by Stephen Mitchell. New York: Random House, 1983.

The Life of the Virgin Mary, translated with an introduction and notes by C. F. MacIntyre. Berkeley: Univ. of California Press, 1947.

The Life of the Virgin Mary, translated with an introduction by Stephen Spender. London: Vision, 1951.

Bibliography

Poems from The Book of Hours, "Das Stundenbuch," translated by Babette Deutsch. Norwalk, Conn.: New Directions, 1941.

Rainer Maria Rilke, Later Poems, translated with an introduction and commentary by J. B. Leishman. London: The Hogarth Press, 1938.

Rainer Maria Rilke, Poems, translated by J. B. Leishman, published by Leonard and Virginia Woolf. London: The Hogarth Press, 1934.

Rainer Maria Rilke, Poems, translated by B. J. Morse. 1941.

Rainer Maria Rilke, Poems, translated by Jessie Lemont. New York: Columbia Univ. Press, 1943. [Reprinted as *154 Selected Lyrics,* London, 1945.]

Rainer Maria Rilke, Poems 1906–26, translated by J. B. Leishman. New York: New Directions, 1956.

Rainer Maria Rilke, Selected Poems, translated by J. B. Leishman. London: The Hogarth Press, 1941. [Reprinted as a Penguin in 1964.]

Rainer Maria Rilke, Selected Poems, translated by Ruth Spiers. Cairo: The Anglo-Egyptian Bookshop, n.d. (ca. 1943).

Rainer Maria Rilke, Selected Poems, translated by Albert Ernest Flemming. New York: Methuen, 1986.

Rainer Maria Rilke, Selected Works, vol. 2, *Poetry,* translated J. B. Leishman. New York: New Directions, 1960.

Rainer Maria Rilke, Poems 1912–1926, selected and translated with an introduction by Michael Hamburger. Redding Ridge, Conn.: Black Swan Books, 1981. [Subtitle on interior leaf: "An Unofficial Rilke."]

Requiem and Other Poems, translated with an introduction by J. B. Leishman. London: The Hogarth Press, 1935.

Requiem for a Woman and Selected Lyric Poems, translated by Andy Gaus, with an introduction by A. S. Wensinger. Putney, Vt.: Threshold Books, 1981.

Rilke: Between Roots, translated by Rika Lesser, with a note by Richard Howard. Princeton, N.J.: Princeton Univ. Press, 1986. [A revision of the limited edition titled *Holding Out,* Omaha: Univ. of Nebraska Press, 1975.]

Rilke on Love and Other Difficulties, translated with a commentary by John J. L. Mood. New York: Norton and Co., 1975.

Rilke's Book of Hours, translated by Anita Barrows and Joanna Macy. New York: Riverhead Books, 1996.

Rilke, The Rose Window and Other Verse from New Poems, selected and illustrated by Ferris Cook. Boston: A Bulfinch Press Book, Little, Brown and Co., 1997.

Bibliography

Selected Poems of Rainer Maria Rilke, translated with commentary by Robert Bly. New York: Harper and Row, 1981. [Includes all of the poems in *The Voices.*]

The Selected Poetry of Rainer Maria Rilke, edited and translated by Stephen Mitchell, with an introduction by Robert Hass. New York: Random House, 1982.

The Tale of the Love and Death of Cornet Christopher Rilke, translated by M. D. Herter Norton. New York: Norton and Co., 1932.

Thirty-One Poems by Rainer Maria Rilke, translated with an introduction by Ludwig Lewisohn. New York: B. Ackermann, 1946.

Translations from the Poetry of Rainer Maria Rilke, by M. D. Herter Norton. New York: Norton and Co., 1938. [Many editions since, 1962, 1993.]

Uncollected Poems, Rainer Maria Rilke, selected and translated by Edward Snow. New York: North Point Press/Farrar, Straus and Giroux, 1996.

The Unknown Rilke, translated by Franz Wright, with an introduction by Egon Schwartz. Oberlin, Ohio: Field Translation Series, 8, 1983.

The Voices, translated by Robert Bly. Denver: Ally Press, 1977. [A ten-poem pamphlet.]

Rilke's French Poems

Saltimbanques, French Prose Poems by Rainer Maria Rilke, translated by A. Poulin, Jr. Port Townsend, Wash.: Graywolf Press, 1978.

The Roses & The Windows, translated by A. Poulin, Jr., with a foreword by W. D. Snodgrass. Port Townsend, Wash.: Graywolf Press, 1980.

The Astonishment of Origins, translated by A. Poulin, Jr. Port Townsend, Wash.: Graywolf Press, 1982.

Orchards, translated by A. Poulin, Jr. Port Townsend, Wash.: Graywolf Press, 1982.

The Migration of Powers, translated by A. Poulin, Jr. Port Townsend, Wash.: Graywolf Press, 1984.

Translations of *The Notebooks of Malte Laurids Brigge*

The Notebook of Malte Laurids Brigge, translated by John Linton. London: The Hogarth Press, 1930.

Bibliography

The Journal of My Other Self, translated by M. D. Herter Norton and John Linton. New York: Norton and Co., 1930.

The Notebooks of Malte Laurids Brigge, translated by M. D. Herter Norton. New York: Norton and Co., 1949.

The Notebooks of Malte Laurids Brigge, translated by Stephen Mitchell. New York: Random House, 1982. [Reprinted in paperback, with an introduction by William H. Gass, New York: Random House, 1985.]

Other Prose

Diaries of a Young Poet, translated by Edward Snow and Michael Winkler. New York: Norton, 1997.

Ewald Tragy, translated by Lola Gruenthal. New York: Twayne, 1958.

Nine Plays, translated by Klaus Phillips and John Locke. New York: Ungar, 1979.

"Preface," translated from the French by Richard Miller, to *Mitsou. Forty Images by Balthus.* New York: Abrams for the Metropolitan Museum of Art, 1984.

Rainer Maria Rilke, Selected Works, vol. 1, *Prose,* translated by G. Craig Houston, with an introduction by J. B. Leishman. New York: New Directions, 1960. [Reprinted as *When Silence Reigns,* with a foreword by Denise Levertov, 1978.]

Rodin, translated by Jesse Lemont and Hans Trausil. New York: Fine Editions Press, 1945. [London edition by Grey Walls Press, 1946, with additional illustrations.] [Unauthorized reprint, Paris: collection "Le Ballet des Muses," Courrier Graphique, n.d.]

Rodin, translated by Robert Firmage. Salt Lake City: Peregrin Smith, 1979. [Richly illustrated.]

Stories of God, translated by M. D. Herter Norton and Nora Purtscher-Wydenbruck, with an introduction by William Rose. London: Sidgwick and Jackson, 1932. [The New York edition by Norton and Co. in the same year has no introduction and lists only Herter Norton as the translator.]

Two Stories of Prague, translated with an introduction by Angela Esterhammer. Hanover, N.H.: Univ. Press of New England, 1994.

Bibliography

Letters

The Letters of Rainer Maria Rilke, 2 vols., translated by Jane Bannard Greene and M. D. Herter Norton. New York: Norton and Co., 1945.

The Letters of Rainer Maria Rilke and Princess Marie von Thurn und Taxis, translated with an introduction by Nora Wydenbruck. New York: New Directions, 1958.

Letters on Cézanne, translated by Joel Agee, with a foreword by Heinrich Wiegand Petzet. New York: Fromm, 1985.

Letters to a Young Poet, translated by M. D. Herter Norton. New York: Norton and Co., 1934, revised ed. 1954, reprinted 1962.

Letters to a Young Poet, translated with an introduction by Stephen Mitchell. New York: Random House, 1984.

Letters to Benvenuta, translated by Heinz Norden, with a foreword by Louis Untermeyer. New York: The Philosophical Library, 1951. [Reprinted by The Hogarth Press in 1953 minus two photographs.]

Letters to Frau Gudi Nölke During His Life in Switzerland, edited with an epilogue and notes by Paul Obermüller, translated by Violet M. Macdonald. London: The Hogarth Press, 1955.

Letters to Merline, 1919–1922, translated by Violet M. Macdonald, with an introduction by J. B. Leishman. London: Methuen and Co., 1951.

Letters to Merline (1919–1922), translated by Jesse Browner from the French edition of 1950, *Lettres Françaises à Merline*. New York: Paragon House, 1989. [Advertised as available in English for the first time in this edition.]

Rainer Maria Rilke: His Last Friendship, unpublished letters to Mrs. Eloui Bey, with a study by Edmond Jaloux. New York: Philosophical Library, 1952. [Translated from the French, *La Dernière Amitie de Rainer Maria Rilke*, by William H. Kennedy.]

Rilke and Benvenuta: An Intimate Correspondence, edited by Magda von Hattingberg, translated by Joel Agee. New York: Fromm Intl., 1987.

Selected Letters of Rilke, edited with an introduction by Harry T. Moore. New York: Anchor Books, 1960.

Selected Letters, 1902–1926, of Rainer Maria Rilke, translated by R. F. C. Hull. London: Macmillan and Co., 1946.

Wartime Letters, 1914–1921, of Rainer Maria Rilke, translated by M. D. Herter Norton. New York: Norton and Co., 1940.

A NOTE ON THE TYPE

This book was set in Fairfield, the first typeface from the hand of the distinguished American artist and engraver Rudolph Ruzicka (1883–1978). In its structure Fairfield displays the sober and sane qualities of the master craftsman whose talent has long been dedicated to clarity. It is the trait that accounts for the trim grace and virility, the spirited design and sensitive balance, of this original typeface.

Rudolph Ruzicka was born in Bohemia and came to America in 1894. He set up his own shop, devoted to wood engraving and printing, in New York in 1913 after a varied career working as a wood engraver, in photoengraving and bank-note printing plants, and as an art director and freelance artist. He designed and illustrated many books, and was the creator of a considerable list of individual prints—wood engravings, line engravings on copper, and aquatints.

Composed by Dix Type, Syracuse, New York
Printed and bound by R. R. Donnelley & Sons,
Harrisonburg, Virginia
Designed by Peter A. Andersen